# RACKS

A natural history must be a vast collection of reliable facts—plus a personality. The facts herein are the best available. Whether the personal touch they bear is acceptable, remains to be seen.

—ERNEST THOMPSON SETON, 1909

# BOOKS BY DAVID PETERSEN

*Big Sky, Fair Land*
  The Environmental Essays of A.B. Guthrie, Jr.

*Among the Elk*
  Wilderness Images

*Among the Aspen*
  A Sylvan Natural History

# RACKS

## The Natural History of Antlers and the Animals That Wear Them

DAVID PETERSEN

*Drawings by*
MICHAEL MCCURDY

CAPRA PRESS
SANTA BARBARA

*For Carolyn*

**Library of Congress Cataloging-in-Publication Data**
Petersen, David.
    Racks : the natural history of antlers and the animals that wear
them / David Petersen ; drawings by Michael McCurdy.
      p.  cm.
    Includes bibliographical references.
    ISBN 0-88496-323-3 : $12.95
    1. Cervidae.  2. Antlers.  3. Wildlife conservation.  I. Title.
QL737.U55P48  1991
599.73'57—dc20                                            91-11391
                                                              CIP

CAPRA PRESS
P.O. Box 2068
Santa Barbara, CA 93120

# Contents

*Acknowledgments* / 6
*Introduction* / 7

I.   OF WHITE TAILS AND MULE EARS / 17
     *The Deer of North America*

II.  THE ELUSIVE WAPITI / 39
     *High, Wide and Handsome*

III. CONSIDER THE COMELY MOOSE / 55
     *No More Mister Nice Guy*

IV.  IN THE LAND OF THE CARIBOU / 65
     *Pleistocene Dreaming*

V.   OF *MEGALOCEROS* AND MIRACLES / 89
     *The Biggest Antlers Ever*

VI.  BIG-ELK STORIES / 103
     *What's in a World Record?*

VII. THE "HORN" TRADE / 115
     *The Good, the Bad, the Misunderstood*

VIII. HOPEFUL MONSTERS / 133
     *A Look at "Freak" Antlers*

*Afterthought*
THE HUNTER AS NATURALIST / 143
     *An Oxymoron?*

*Appendices*
A.  Cervid Taxonomy: The Deer Family Tree / 158
B.  Deer and Elk Conservation Organizations / 161
C.  Crockett & Boone Club Scoring System / 165

*Bibliography* / 175

# Acknowledgments

It is one of the unfortunate aspects of research biology that so very much of the often keenly interesting information and speculation generated by field and laboratory workers never gets relayed to the interested lay public—not, at least, in an understandable, much less enjoyable, fashion. Consequently, I am honored to have this opportunity to pass along a cross-section of the knowledge and sense of wonder that has been brought to light through ongoing and painstaking scientific studies of the antlered species.

To the Drs. Anthony and George Bubenik, Valerius Geist, Gary Wolfe and the other experts in the fields of antler and cervid study who have so generously provided information, criticism and encouragement during the preparation of this book, I acknowledge a great debt of gratitude.

I wish also to thank the several anonymous academic and scientific readers who offered valuable, though not always charitable or welcome, suggestions for the improvement of the book-in-progress; Betti Albrecht and Gregory McNamee, for their generous and expert advice; A. B. Guthrie, Jr., Edward Abbey and Ernest Thompson Seton, my exemplars; Noel Young, who knows how to make good things happen fast in the slow world of book publishing; Carolyn, my live-in editor; and *Bugle* and *Mother Earth News* magazines, in whose pages some bits of this book appeared originally.

# Introduction

ONCE, LONG AGO and far away, I was the managing editor of a touring cyclists' magazine in southern California. One of my most enjoyable duties there—because it allowed me to get out of my windowless office and travel, at someone else's expense, no less—was riding to and reporting on some of the dozens of cycle rallies held throughout North America each year. In pursuit of this happy chore, one September morning in 1978, I was riding the return leg of a mad-dash roundabout to Vancouver, British Columbia (via Tijuana, Mexico), having just emerged from the southern end of the gloriously undulating Big Sur stretch of California Highway 1.

Somewhere north of San Simeon, near the sprawling, verdant Hearst estate, where the terrain seaward of the highway tumbles in crumbling vertical cliffs down to a rocky beach, and the grasslands to the east roll gently off toward distant timbered hills, the three of them approached the road.

Knowing nothing much about elk beyond the fact that they resembled very large deer, I was surprised and delighted, though perhaps not amazed, to see a bull, a cow and a leggy calf traveling together. A family, I remember thinking, ingenuous in my ignorance. A perfect little family of elk.

As my humming Yamaha (motorcycles rarely rumble these days) narrowed the distance between the animals and me, the bull, with six long tines sprouting from each treelike main antler beam, glided over the barbed-wire fence paralleling the highway and shot across the asphalt a scant few yards away.

There was no other traffic in sight, so I braked to a stop and killed the engine, right there in the middle of the road. Now

7

the cow also leapt the fence, but hesitated to cross the highway, waiting with obvious anxiety for her deer-sized calf to follow. But the fence was rather more of an obstacle to the calf than it had been for the adults. Growing frantic (no doubt abetted by my threatening proximity), the calf minced back and forth along the fence, as if looking for an opening through which to slip or a low spot over which to bound. Finding neither, the youngster finally bucked up his courage and made the jump, clearing the fence handily from a standing start.

Her progeny again safely in tow, the cow and her calf hurriedly crossed the road close in front of me and rejoined the bull, who'd been waiting nearby and somewhat less than patiently. Reunited, the trio trotted off toward the sea cliffs and disappeared over the edge, following, I presumed, a familiar trail leading down to the beach. Headed, one might guess, for a surfside picnic of shore grasses and wildflowers. The encounter had lasted, start to finish, less than a handful of minutes.

Continuing my homeward journey, I reflected on the grace under pressure shown by those three animals. And I thought a lot about the bull's massive, beautifully symmetrical antlers. Never had I seen a deer that wore such a rack and carried itself so regally as had that big bull elk. A photographic memory of the animal sailing so effortlessly over the fence, his great white antlers glinting with reflected sunlight, was etched indelibly into my smog-muddled brain.

Back home, I hied to the public library to learn something of elk in general and the incredible antlers of the males in particular. Only then, amidst stacks of literature—some biological and technical, some merely colorful and interesting—did I realize how fortuitous that Big Sur encounter had been.

First, the Tule elk—to which race my three passing acquaintances belonged—is the smallest-bodied and rarest of the four North American elk subspecies, with no more than a few hundred of the animals living in small pockets scattered around central and northern California at the time of our meeting. (As of 1991, the population had grown to around

2,500.) The statistical probability of a chance close encounter such as the one I'd enjoyed was minuscule.

From the library books I also learned that September is the month of rut, the mating season for elk. It is then that mature males bugle and spar to establish a breeding hierarchy. Those bulls who dominate in these contests, having demonstrated their physical and genetic superiority, then go about gathering into harems as many cows as each can attract and hoard away from his rivals. Most often, cows towing the previous spring's young will temporarily evict their calves as they approach ovulation. Thus, September is not exactly a family time of year for elk. For that matter, no time is; bull elk rarely show anything resembling familial behavior or actively participate in the rearing of the young—a trait common among most mammalian species, humans not excepted.

I was left to conclude that my Big Sur bull, at that fairly early stage in the rut (which typically peaks as September becomes October), had so far managed to collect only the one cow. And the cow, still a fortnight or so away from ovulation, had yet to shoo away her calf.

My pretty but ignorantly anthropomorphic vision of a perfect little "family" of elk was smashed. Rather than cherishing and protecting the calf, the bull was, in all likelihood, merely tolerating its presence in hopes of enjoying the sexual favors of its mother (a circumstance sadly common in human society as well).

No matter, for I was hooked on antlers and the animals that wear them thenceforth and, it appears from here, forever. In the dozen years since that brief sighting, I've spent thousands of hours poking into the natural histories and spying on the everyday lives of North America's four glorious antler bearers— elk, deer, moose and caribou; the family Cervidae. To better indulge this growing interest (though certainly not for that reason alone), I picked up and moved, a decade or so ago, to the San Juan Mountains of southwestern Colorado.

Here, the winters are long and frequently hard, the economy is thin and seasonal, and making a living is far from easy. But in this place I am constantly near nature, viewing deer and elk on an almost daily basis.

To observe moose—a species conspicuously absent hereabouts (but, it is rumored, due to be introduced nearby "some day soon")—I make almost-annual treks to our northern national parks: Glacier, Grand Teton, Yellowstone. Caribou, however, remained for me a frustrating abstract until, in September of 1988, I finally realized a longstanding dream of visiting the backcountry of Alaska during the annual caribou migration. One such trip, I recall thinking beforehand, would last for a lifetime. I was wrong. To a big game freak, Alaska is the most muscular of magnets.

Through all of this I've learned—what? I have learned that, even now, I know very little about those great mysteries of form and function, function and form, that we call antlers. (The word derives from the Latin *anteoculare*, meaning "before the eyes.") But in this relative ignorance I am not alone, for even the world's leading antler researchers freely admit that they, too, know little, in absolute terms, about the more esoteric workings of what the scientific community terms "antlerogenesis"—the processes of evolution, development, growth, social employment, annual casting off and rapid regeneration of antlers. Little, that is, compared to all that remains shrouded in mystery. And I have also learned—to trot out an obedient cliché of universal academic application—that for every question answered, several more invariably arise.

How, for instance, did antlers evolve? Why, when and how did the evolutionary process begin? How and why do antlers grow, fall off and regrow annually—an accomplishment unparalleled in the entire mammalian world? How do antlers differ from horns? Why are caribou the only deer species whose females regularly grow antlers? What accounts for the incredible diversity of antler shape and size between species? What are the causes of nontypical, or "freak" antlers?

These questions and more, if unable always to answer outright, I will in the following pages at least explore to the limits of established fact, likely probability and pregnant hypothesis.

A few orienting words concerning the latter: Hypothesis is exactly what its name implies—a promising hypothetical. And evolutionary science, as it strives to interpret events that unfolded in the almost unimaginably distant past, while plainly valid, is decidedly hypothetical. How can we know *absolutely* what did or did not transpire millions of years ago? We can't. Researchers can gather and analyze evidence, propose theories and hypotheses based on that evidence, and apply scientific method to test the validity of those theories and hypotheses . . . but they, and we, will never, ever know with dead certainty the exact progression of events that unfolded or the precise doings of animals that lived and died in millennia long past.

Still, educated speculation is great good fun. To maintain some sense of balance, I have attempted here to present—if not all—at least some of the most intriguing points of tenacious academic contention. If I should give more weight to one idea than another, as I sometimes shall, I do so openly—and isn't that the writer's privilege, perhaps even his duty?

Please, then, accept the various hypotheses presented herein as I offer them—not as the final word, nor even, in all cases, as current scientific consensus, but merely as sound and compelling ruminations. From there, you are invited to take the cud and chew it yourself, to use my collected research and speculation as a catalyst for your own further self-education—and, of course, to reach your own conclusions.

🐚

In the course of researching an earlier natural history (*Among the Elk*, Northland Publishing, 1988), I gained the acquaintance of several leading researchers in various fields of antler study. From these experts I got not only frank critiques of my manuscripts and definitive answers to my pesky and sometimes ignorant questions about elk, but also a sense that the mystery of antlers was a story waiting to be told. For, unlike many fields of biological science, the serious study of antlers is relatively young. Further, most of what *is* known has been published—if at all and up to now—only in highly technical scientific theses, dissertations, texts, journals and monographs.

It was exactly this set of charming circumstances that precipitated the undertaking of this book.

*Racks* is, to my knowledge, unique in that it is the first and sole effort to present in a detailed, technically accurate yet easily digestible and perhaps even modestly entertaining manner, the highlights of and speculations arising from expert research into the natural history of antlers and the animals that wear them. My prime hope for this book is that it will lead you to share my sense of wonder for those marvelous sculptures of nature popularly referred to—always with a sense of awe and respect—as *Racks*.

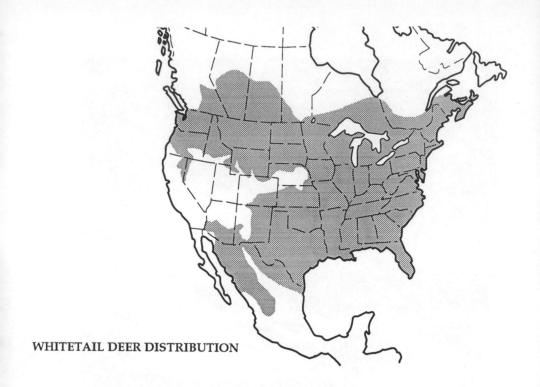

**WHITETAIL DEER DISTRIBUTION**

**MULE DEER DISTRIBUTION**

# I

# OF WHITE TAILS AND MULE EARS
## *The Deer of North America*

> Everywhere some species of deer seems to
> be at home . . . it is always invincibly graceful,
> and adds beauty and animation to every
> landscape,—a charming animal, and a great
> credit to nature.
>
> —JOHN MUIR

A GOLDEN SEPTEMBER morning.

I am sitting still as a stump near the crest of a Rocky Mountain ridgetop at 9,000 feet elevation. My back is propped against the gnarly trunk of an ancient ponderosa pine, my senses as tuned and alert as they can be this early in the day—watching, listening, waiting.

The roosters were still dreaming of fat friendly hens when I crawled some hours ago from the womblike warmth of my bed and began the hike up through four miles of star-spangled darkness, my goal being to gain this familiar overlook by dawn. That much I have accomplished.

I have come to this place in hopes of seeing elk. Upon topping the ridge overlooking a sprawling grove of quaking aspens and, below and beyond that, a wide grassy park, I crept to this vantage and sat myself down. I've been sitting here motionless for more than an hour now, watching the world brighten before me as the morning sun scales the eastern sky, its energy crawling warm and welcome up my aching back.

Coyotes—their wavering, quavering, intermingling voices howling out racket enough for a full choir, though they are probably but a duo—sing briefly from an unknown distance, announcing yet again to the world that, as it is said, sunrise has failed to slip past them unnoticed.

Nearer, somewhere down in the autumn-gold aspens, a bull elk bugles. I tense and strain my eyes, fully expecting to see him wander into the open at any moment, the visible vapor of his breath jetting in twin streams from flared nostrils, the animal hot into the rut, looking for trouble, looking for love. The bull bugles a couple of times more in the next half hour, but remains hidden and soon falls silent.

In the renewed quiet, I shift my attention to a small sound I've been hearing off and on since first light, coming from somewhere, maybe everywhere, and quite nearby—a constant, high-pitched, low-volume peeping similar to that made by contented chickadees. Yet different. And this peeping comes not from the trees above, but from the earth around me.

I peer about, poking visually into the various sere clumps of grass from which the birdlike music seems to emanate, but spot nothing. After a while I give it up and return to watching the park below for elk.

But the peeping gradually becomes more incessant, reclaiming my attention, beckoning me to look. And looking, I see at last the tiny music's source. A bit of movement in the grass just to my front. A minuscule dark form—something of the order Rodentia scales one of my oiled leather boots, hesitates, then ventures up along the ankle and races up a green wool trouser leg toward a bony knee. Suddenly, seeming at last to have realized its error and peril, the little creature leaps to the other leg and darts back down to Mother Earth, homeostasis and safety.

The temerarious scout having landed safely, more of the little creatures soon reveal themselves. They are shrews, among the world's smallest and most ancient mammals. Their tiny bodies are cloaked in fur as dark and rich as mink, their eyes shining like minute black pearls set in long, pointy, fearful faces.

Suddenly they are everywhere, hurrying to and fro beneath the scant grassy cover, a veritable swarming of shrews. The scout that scaled my leg apparently has passed the word, correctly, that I am nothing to fear, a mere misshapen outgrowth of the tree against which I lean. Even so, none approach me. I watch their antics for a while longer, then, giving in to an ornery impulse, jerk one knee. Terrified, the shrew crew scatters and falls silent.

I've often heard, but until this moment have found it hard to comprehend, that populations of shrews and other small rodents can at times soar into the thousands per acre. Now, being shown, I believe. I smile, having thoroughly enjoyed this impromptu educational experience, thankful for this bit of new shrew knowledge. This, also, is a part of the natural experience, an important and enchanting part too often overlooked by the amateur naturalist in his compulsive search for the large, the strikingly beautiful, the grand.

At about eight, the sweet monotony of this tranquil morning is again disrupted—this time more profoundly—when a mule deer doe steps lightly from a nearby jungle of Gambel's* oak and ventures onto the edge of a small clearing between us. Her sudden appearance is as silent as thought, as unexpected as epiphany. I welcome the visitation. Few wild animals I have known are as curious, intrepid, entertaining, unpredictable as an unfrightened doe, and this little muley miss looks to be no exception.

From her position of relative safety at the edge of the head-high patch of oak, the doe now steps tentatively forward, stopping midway in the clearing, less than twenty yards to my front. I make no sound louder than the tom-tom beating of my heart, there is no wind to betray me to her keen nostrils, and even though she twice peers directly at me, her big brown eyes fail to recognize my camouflaged form as human, frozen here as I am like an aging bearded Buddha.

---

* *Quercas gambellii* —the double-i indicates the possessive form.

Outwardly, the doe appears calm. Yet she seems somehow pensive, distracted, neglectful of her instinctive concern for potential danger to her front. Instead, her interest seems focused primarily to her rear. She ventures another step in my direction, stops, twists long, gracile neck back over tawny shoulder to look, listen. Her big jackrabbit ears pivot this way and that, that way and this, each independent in its movements from the other.

Now, from the northwest, sliding down the doe's back trail and up behind her, comes a brief cool breeze. The long thin muzzle comes suddenly up. Palpitating nostrils taste the air. She tenses, stamps the ground. The muscles under her sleek pelage quiver visibly. The breeze dies. The doe relaxes and glides on across the clearing, shying off the game trail and down the hill, away from me, submerging again into the ubiquitous oak brush.

As ephemeral and puzzling as a dream, the doe has come and gone within the span of a couple of minutes, leaving me to ponder the enigma of her strange behavior.

I'm still trying to make the pieces fit, thinking about maybe following her trail to spy, when a subtle something flickers in the periphery of my vision. Moving only my eyes, I shift my gaze and see, screened behind a confusion of red-leafed oak branches, near the very spot where the little doe had first appeared, the large head and thick ivory antlers of what seems to be a medium-sized bull elk. A shot of adrenaline jolts me. I hold my breath.

After glancing back over his shoulder, much as the doe had done, the antlered animal strides out into the clearing. My vision no longer obstructed, I see immediately that this is no ordinary bull elk. In fact, it's no elk at all, but an elk-sized mule deer buck.

Perhaps, I consider, the enigmatic doe was walking point for this patriarch—a hypothesis which, if correct, would account not only for her inordinate interest in her back trail, but also for this big buck's relaxed confidence. On the other hand, the beginning of the November rutting season for mule deer is still several weeks away, and bucks this time of year normally do not keep company with does, but run in bachelor groups of two to six animals. And why, also, if this buck is the follower and not the followed, is he, like the doe before him, so obviously concerned with where he has just been?

As the animal approaches, I get a better look at his antlers. Throbbing as I am with the debilitating chemical ailment hunters call "buck fever," it fails to occur to me to count tines; I'm too taken by the *gestalt,* or totality, of this great beast's headgear to notice anything more specific than *big, wide, tall, thick, heavy, beautiful.* In an instant the critical moment is passed; the buck turns down the hill away from me—if not following the doe, at least taking the same invisible trail. This new course presents a posterior rather than a frontal view and is rapidly increasing the distance between me and this "trophy"-quality animal.

My thoughts leap to a book containing vertical columns of figures. I harbor strongly mixed feelings about the ultimate value, even the morality, of such potentially macho-competitive, anthropocentric constructs as big game record books. I recall the words of poet-novelist Jim Harrison, who once wrote that, beyond the point of gaining competence in the basic skills . . .

> Any spirit of competition in hunting or fishing
> dishonors the prey. It means that you are either
> unaware of, or have no feeling toward, your
> fellow creatures. . . . Competition also engenders
> anger, and there's little point in being out in the
> forest . . . if you're going to be pissed off.

Yet, both the Boone and Crockett and Pope and Young clubs have nothing but the best of intentions and have in fact done a great deal of good work toward improving the ethics of hunters. And one of the best men I've known—honest to a fault, sensitive, generous—is a high-ranking official within the Pope and Young Club. As in other areas of human endeavor, the whole, I reckon, can't be held responsible for the sins of a few. And too, for an antler fanatic like me, the books and the facts they contain are fascinating.

In any event, I now find myself thinking through a litany of remembered measurements and mental photographs, comparing, wondering. There can be no doubt, I conclude, that this buck would rank high, mighty high indeed, in the B&C, P&Y or any other antler rating scheme. But, somewhat oddly given that I'm a hunter, I have no urge to be the one to list this buck's stats in those morbidly fascinating pages.

Each September I take bow and arrows in hand and perform an almost ritualistic hunt, stretching it out for as long as I can, searching for meat, knowledge and, it is mine to hope, humility. My kind of hunting is something I find difficult to explain and certainly don't feel obliged to justify to anyone who doesn't already understand, hunter or not. But I also hold an aficionado's respect for the special in nature. Some things are just too grand, too fine, too rare to destroy. Even had I come here in search of my winter's supply of venison—a highly valued commodity in our hungry larder—I'd like to think I would let this particular buck live.

Let him live in the conviction that greater pleasure is to be gained just knowing that such a masterpiece of evolution roams across the mottled greens and browns of this special place so near my home. Knowing that—even as I split firewood in my front yard, or sit in my chair and read, or make love—this superb animal drinks from the little mountain brook sliding through the valley below . . . the selfsame brook at which I knelt and drank earlier this morning.

Let him live in the hope that he will follow, court and make fawns with the enigmatic doe and her sisters. To kill an animal as rare and fine as this one, I reflect, would be to rob this place of the special magic his living presence grants it. But, then again, I have not come here today in search of venison—a fat young fork-horn buck is already in my freezer—and probably merely delude myself.

These high-flown thoughts suddenly evaporate when another deer appears. The departing buck, spotting this new arrival at the same instant I do, stops, turns back. For a few moments both animals are in clear view, and I see that the second is even heavier of body and more magnificent of rack than the first. And now—I'll be damned—a *third* buck materializes from the seemingly pregnant oak brush island. And this one . . . my God; he is grand beyond the telling. Never have I seen such a rack or even dreamed that such a deer exists. He is the quintessence of deerness, the epitome of buckness, the apogee of wildness.

These three animals obviously are a bachelor group, traveling together, albeit loosely at the moment, for company and practice. Sparring practice, that is—those low-intensity, low-risk, mock antler battles and shoving matches that help to establish a pecking order among peer bucks. One bachelor group may be composed of nothing but fork-horns (two points per antler beam) and spikes (a single unforked shaft per side). Meanwhile, the really big boys, such as these three I'm gawking at now, form elite and aloof clubs of their own. Come the rut, all within a given group will know full well who's honcho, *el segundo* and right on down the line. This saves a great deal of time, energy and potential injury when the serious rutting competition begins.

Somewhere down the mountain, from beyond the aspen grove and out past the verdant park, a bull elk bugles. Probably the same one I heard earlier. He sounds to be moving away.

Living as I do in country rich in both elk and mule deer, my sense of the magnificence of the smaller and more plentiful deer has gradually become overshadowed by the mystery and singular grandeur of the larger and scarcer elk. Not only is the average elk some three times bigger than the average muley, but the wapiti is also more elusive, less often seen, a hermit of the most rugged and secluded redoubts these rocky old mountains can provide; the wailing spirit-being of the high country.

And so it has evolved in recent years that I am all but single-minded in my focus on elk. Too often, I pay little more heed to the deer I spook into flight as I walk, or to those that drift by me unaware and unalarmed as I stand or sit camouflaged and motionless, than I do to the ubiquitous pine squirrels scolding from the trees.

But now, in these few precious moments here on this high ridgetop on this chill autumn morning, nothing else matters to me, not a thing in the entire world, beyond this trio of antlered masterworks walking insouciantly out of my view, out of my life.

As nearly as science has been able to determine, antlers and the animals that wear them got their start some twenty-five million years ago, near the opening of that highly fruitful epoch of mammalian development, the Miocene.

Over much of the earth, this was a time of tropical and semitropical climates. Nurtured by a natural greenhouse of humidity and warmth, plant growth was rampant. The largest group of Miocene ungulates, the order of even-toed hooved animals called Artiodactyla, was represented primarily by hornless, antlerless animals small enough to maneuver easily through this dense tropical jungle.

There is much to be learned by comparing the anatomies of these early ungulates, based on their fossil remains, to the skeletal structures of their modern descendants. By cataloging the social behavior of living animals and taking it to be similar to that of certain anatomically related extinct species, evolutionary biologists judge that most Miocene ungulate types—given especially the density of the cover in which they lived—probably kept to themselves within the bounds of relatively limited personal territories, rather than roaming far and wide in herds. In this respect, they were more like the whitetail deer than the caribou we know today.

Such social aloofness, if it in fact existed, would have been entirely practical, in that it's at best difficult for a large group of wild animals to keep together in thick cover. Even in the course of normal daily activities such as feeding, groups would tend to drift apart and have difficulty reassembling due to restricted visibility and hampered communications. During panicked flight from predators, maintaining group cohesion would be all but impossible; the herd would be scattered like a covey of quail.

Thus, it is hypothesized, the Miocene ungulates living in dense forest understory and along its brushy edges came to be loners. To defend their feeding and breeding territories against others of their species, these small, innocuous mammals had, variously and only, hooves for kicking, elongated upper canine teeth for biting and thick-skulled heads for butting.

Dr. Anthony "Tony" Bubenik, one of the world's leading authorities on antlers, the animals that wear them and their co-evolution, now living in Canada—and his son, Dr. George Bubenik, professor of biology at the University of Guelph, Ontario, also a leading antler expert—spoke with me recently about the significance of instinctive head-butting as they judge it to have affected the initial appearance of the precursors of horns and antlers. The essence of their explanation is as follows:

The initial stimulus for the development of horns in bovids (cattle, sheep, goats and bison) may have been an inherited genetic programming (instinct) for head-butting during territorial and breeding disputes—a behavior still strongly displayed among many bovids today, most notably the bighorn sheep, *Ovis canadensis*. The minor injuries received via these head-knocking contests could have triggered in certain randomly occurring, "genetically fortunate" animals the release of a freak potential for growth abnormalities in the form of hard nodules—"bumpers," as it were—in the skin overlying the skull.

Under the refining pressure of competition, any animal that was genetically inclined to develop even small skull bumps at points of likely contact during head-butting contests would have had something of a physical—and therefore, via intimidation, also social—advantage over others of the same species. This enhanced social standing, no matter how slight, would have improved the bumpy-headed individual's survival and breeding opportunities, helping to reinforce its eccentric genes within the local population, thus encouraging repeated occurrences of similar cranial abnormalities in subsequent generations. Given time, and via the workings of natural selection, the bumps could have begun to appear without the stimulus of head injury.

But that proposal, even should it be accurate, accounts only for horns. What of antlers? Even though horns and antlers both are located on the head and are superficially similar in appearance, the Drs. Bubenik caution that the two should not be thought of as being related, either structurally or developmentally. Even though the precursors of horns appeared some three million years before the forerunners of antlers, and in related species, antlers should not be thought of as having evolved *from* horns.

How, then, might have antlers begun?

Since modern cervids lack an instinct for head-butting, we can presume the same for their forebears of Miocene vintage. (It is true that male deer of all species make antler contact during greeting ceremonies, sparring contests and rutting battles, but this social behavior develops gradually, with the onset of puberty, and is not true instinctive head-butting; whereas bovids knock noggins almost from birth.)

Rather than instinctive head-butting, the initial stimulus for antler development in deer, the Bubeniks offer, may have been *accidental* head injury—such as hoof-blows received during territorial and breeding disputes, or scalp lacerations incurred while running full-out and headlong through heavy underbrush during flight from predators.

Only one thing is certain—we will never know for sure. Perhaps the Bubeniks' (and others') intriguing ideas are right on the money—and perhaps head-butting and accidental injuries had nothing whatsoever to do with it. Perhaps it was all mere serendipity. But the bumps nonetheless appeared, and we have fossil evidence to help track what transpired next.

While similar in both location on the head and perhaps even initial growth stimulus, early cervid skull knobs, called "peduncles," were anatomically different from the bumps, or "dermal ossicones," of the bovids. Rather than being floating buttons of bone attached to the skull only by cartilage and overlying skin, as were the bovid ossicones, peduncles were living, skin-covered *outgrowths of the skull,* which developed in the prefrontal periosteum—a fibrous tissue covering the external surfaces of all bones.

An old-line and widely respected hypothesis holds that peduncles would have served much the same social purposes as did early horns, providing defensive shields against head injury. Offensively, peduncled animals would have had a modest new form of weapon that could be used at least to intimidate, if not actually to injure, bareheaded or smaller-peduncled competitors of the same species. Therefore, so this "weaponry" approach to antler development postulates, peduncled animals would have enjoyed a slight advantage in survival and breeding, passing along their peduncle-prone genes to future generations—separate from but more-or-less in parallel with the way horns had earlier evolved among the bovids. (Should you be interested in pursuing this intriguing school of thought further, a strong case for the weaponry theory, at least as it applies to the European red deer, is made by Timothy Clutton-Brock in his book, *The Red Deer.*) But not all evolutionary biologists agree with this scenario, and any informed opinion rates a forum here. In a scientific paper titled "The Behavioral Aspects of Antlerogenesis," (translated from the German-language scientific journal *Saugetier-kundliche Mitteilungen*), Tony Bubenik has this to say on the subject:

> [My] behavioral observations do not support
> the notion that the ultimate cause of antler
> evolution was the development of weaponry,
> whether of offensive, defensive or mixed design.
> Comparisons of fossil . . . antlers and the use of
> antlers in living species support the idea that

> antlers were selected for symbolic functions,
> such as . . . individual advertisements to
> demonstrate maturity . . . and individual status,
> that is, rank within the social class.

In our correspondence, Dr. Bubenik added that "The primary social advantages of peduncles were to facilitate discrimination between sexes and social class or rank. Among same-species animals that knew each other, peduncles substituted for 'proper names.' Thus, in my and others' views, the use of antlers as weapons came as a later, acquired utility."

Agreeing with this interpretation, the younger of the two Drs. Bubenik offers that "Further evidence that antlers did not develop primarily as weapons is in their shape. The pattern of branching is such that it minimizes the chance of injury, rather than enhancing it, during conflicts. The shapes are perfect for sparring, not spearing.

"Additionally, the inborn head movements of various deer males during presentation to a rival emphasize the most impressive components of the antlers: that is, the "royals" in elk and [its Old World cousin, the] red deer, and the palms of fallow deer, caribou and moose. This indicates that the purpose of antlers is to intimidate, not to provoke a fight."

Whatever the prime mover, once the genetic ball was tossed into play, natural selection stepped in to manipulate—in some cases to reinforce, though in most to cancel—the tendency for the continued growth and refinement of peduncles.

To take the Bubeniks' ideas one step further, as I understand them: When an expressed genetic potential (in this case, peduncles) proves to be important to the survival and betterment of the individual in which it appears—and therefore, over the long haul, potentially (albeit inadvertently) to the species as well—it can then develop independently of the original growth stimulus. Thus, while accidental head injuries may or may not have initiated growth of the very first peduncles in "freak" individuals possessing the genetic potential for such growth, the use of these new organs as an enhanced mechanism for scent communication is the most

likely candidate to have kept their recurrence and enlarge-
ment in play, providing the evolutionary justification for
continued development toward modern antlers.

How might this phenomenon have worked?

The Bubeniks offer a possibility: Scent glands located at the
tips of skin-covered peduncles could have developed the
ability to produce sexually exciting aromas, or pheromones. If
so, these scents would have been emitted at the perfect height
(approximately nose level) for reception by "conspecifics," or
members of the same species. Supporting this theory is the fact
that even though the mature, hardened antlers of modern deer
do not contain scent glands, the skinlike velvet overlying
*developing* antlers in fact does. Ontogeny recapitulating
phylogeny?

George Bubenik elucidates: "The pheromone-related
'advertising' function of antlers might have been more
pronounced in early ancestors of the cervids, but even today,
antler velvet contains the highest concentration of sebaceous
[oil producing] glands found in deer skin. These glands are
under testosterone control and during the maximal production
period (shortly before velvet shedding) the amount of oily
substance [sebum] on the velvet hair is sometimes so great that
it becomes visible as small droplets. At this time bucks are
already searching for available does and perhaps the smell of
the secretion may help them to make contact."

In addition to the scents contained in the sebum produced
by living velvet, the males of modern deer species, once the
velvet is shed from their newly formed antlers, display a strong
urge to impregnate the bare antlers with pheromones. This
they accomplish by rubbing their preorbital glands (two
slitlike openings located just below the eyes) on trees and
brush, then scraping their antlers over these stains to pick up
the scent. Some male cervids also urinate directly on their
antlers (during the rut, the urine of all deer species is rich in
pheromones) or, as in the case of elk, into mud holes, or
"wallows," which they then plow and stir with their antlers
and roll in bodily.

Early peduncles probably were skin-covered and perennial (worn year-round). But unlike horns, which, in the majority of cases, are grown by both bovid sexes, (albeit in generally reduced size and ornateness in females), peduncles are thought to have developed only on males. According to the Bubeniks, given time and natural selection's stamp of approval, the peduncles of some species gradually enlarged and took on varying forms that reflected the age, physical condition and social status of their wearers.

And so it was, the Drs. Bubenik believe, that peduncles, in addition to being scent transmitters, gradually became visual indicators that would allow one male to judge, *without the need to engage in life-threatening physical conflict,* the relative combat prowess of his rutting competitors. Perhaps even more important, females would then have had an instantaneous and accurate visual yardstick by which to compare the physical and genetic worth of their various suitors.

At least hypothetically, then, in the various species destined to become deer, peduncles at some point may have assumed three of the very tasks that today are handled by antlers: scent dispersal, visual symbolism and intraspecific (within the same species) defense/offense. Each of these tasks, you will note, is social in nature. (By contrast, the "functional" organs, such as nose, eyes and ears, enable an animal to find food and avoid danger.)

For a long, slow time, peduncle development remained almost static. It was "only" eight to twelve million years ago that something new and dramatic finally began happening with peduncles: In some species, they sprouted small, bony, skinless, deciduous (shed and regrown annually) projections at their tips. At first, these projections were modest, equal to or less than the lengths of the skin-covered peduncles from which they sprouted. But with time, lots of it, they grew and gradually evolved into the varied and often magnificent organs we know today as antlers. Again, George Bubenik amplifies:

"The capability to cast [and annually regrow] antlers came with the increased sensitivity of antlers to male sex hormones, causing the proximal portions [lowest, located nearest the skull] to become mineralized [hardened] to the point of 'petrification'. Thus, after the annual useful period for antlers had passed, the organs were discarded.

"The advantage in discarding the old and growing new antlers each year is that it provides the capability of annually changing antler size and shape to correspond to changes in body condition. In this way, when a breeding-age male is strong, he produces impressive antlers that advertise his prowess; when he grows weaker [through injury, disease, starvation or old age], he produces smaller antlers that indicate he is out of the competition and thus will not provoke antagonism from a superior rival. The bovids [with their permanent horns] do not have this flexibility."

At and subsequent to the time in evolution where they became the bases from which antlers annually spring, the bony, skin-covered skull projections of deer cease to be called peduncles, and are referred to instead as "pedicles" (pronounced to rhyme with medicals), about which more later.

Deer, with or without antlers, are strange and wonderful creatures.

The "true" deer genus, *Odocoileus,* comprises just two species in North America—the whitetails (*O. virginianus*), and the mule deer (*O. hemionus*). The Columbian blacktail of the northern Pacific coastal states and British Columbia (*O. h. columbianus*) is a slightly smaller regional variation of the mule deer, having evolved sufficient individuality to be considered a bona-fide subspecies. A third prominent member of the mule deer clan is the Sitka blacktail (*O. h. sitkensis*) of coastal British Columbia and Alaska plus various of their offshore islands. It's a close relative of the Columbian blacktail.

While there are seventeen recognized subspecies of whitetail and eight of mule deer presently living above the Mexican border (with several more of each type below), the four just named—Virginia whitetail, Rocky Mountain mule deer, coastal blacktail and Sitka—are the most common and best known.

It has been guesstimated that before the arrival of Europeans, North America may have supported as many as forty million whitetails and ten million mule deer. But by 1908—due to habitat lost to human settlement and, more abrupt in its effects, the mass slaughter of millions of deer for their hides alone (which were valued at as little as two bits each)—America's deer population had plummeted to a scant half million, all species combined. That's a ninety-five percent loss. Fortunately, with the last-minute implementation and aggressive enforcement of protective measures, extinction was prevented.

Through the workings of innovative game management programs financed almost exclusively by special taxes imposed on hunters, our deer population has rallied in the past half century to the point where, according to recent estimates of the Wildlife Management Institute in Washington, D.C., the U.S. (including Alaska and Hawaii) now supports some 12.5 to fourteen million whitetail and 4.5 to seven million mule deer . . . seventeen to twenty-one million total, or roughly forty percent of the estimated 'pre-Columbian bounty.

The whitetail is most abundant in the midwestern and eastern United States, though none of the contiguous forty-eight is totally devoid of the species, and the only states lacking self-sustaining populations are California, Nevada and Utah. In conjunction with its ubiquity, the whitetail's skill at surviving and even prospering in largely deforested agricultural areas and on the very fringes of—in fact, *within*—human popula- tion centers, makes it the most commonly sighted (and photographed, and hunted, and run-over) big game animal in North America today.

Although whitetails may seem fairly large when viewed from a distance, mature bucks rarely stand much higher than three-and-a-half feet at the shoulders. Live weights average around 150 pounds (68 kilograms) but occasionally range much higher. In point of astonishing fact, according to naturalist-photographer Leonard Lee Rue III, who has a marvelous talent for sleuthing out such interesting details, the heaviest whitetail buck on record was killed by a Minnesota hunter back in 1926, weighed 402 pounds (183 kg) eviscerated and would have gone an estimated 511 pounds (232 kg) on the hoof. That's approaching the size of a cow elk or a caribou bull. Additionally, several other northeastern whitetails have weighed in excess of four hundred live pounds (182 kg).

The whitetail's most striking physical characteristic, aside from the heavy antlers of the mature bucks, is the feature from which it takes its common name. Although the foot-long tail of *O. virginianus* is predominantly brown on its top, or outer side, its underside is as pure a white as occurs in nature. When the tail is held close against the rump, as it usually is, only a border of white is visible and the animal remains fairly well camouflaged. But when the tail is erected to expose its snowy underside in conjunction with a large white rump patch, we see the striking "flag" for which this species is famous.

Leaving the East and Midwest to the whitetail, the mule deer is a dyed-in-the-fur westerner, its range extending from southeastern Alaska well down into Mexico, and from the Pacific Coast eastward to a north-south line angling from Hudson Bay in Canada down through central Texas. Notwithstanding a handful of whopper whitetails that may outweigh even the biggest mule deer, the muley, on the average, is the largest-bodied of the *Odocoileus* genus. Adult bucks commonly weigh 150 to two hundred pounds (68 to 91 kg) or more, with does being noticeably smaller (as holds true for all deer species).

In physical form and antler conformation, think of small muleys and you have a fair image of the near-twin blacktail types, the Sitka being somewhat more diminutive than the coastal. But while the muley's tail is narrow and black only toward the end, blacktail tails are broad and, save for a thin white fringe, display a universal dark brown to black from root to tip.

It's obvious from which end blacktails and whitetails get their common names, but the muley's moniker hails from an anterior distinction: huge, mulish ears that work after the fashion of dish antennae to gather in from great distances even the faintest of sounds.

Another way in which the muley differs from the whitetail is in style of high-gear locomotion. The whitetail runs by pushing off alternately with front and rear legs in long, graceful bounds. A mule deer in a hurry, however, prefers to launch itself with all four legs at once in pogo-stick leaps that verge on the comical, each bound seeming to gain more altitude than forward distance. This peculiar gait is sometimes referred to as "stotting," a term commonly applied to the similar bouncing run of certain African antelopes.

Theories vary concerning the evolutionary value—that is, the survival advantange—of stotting: perhaps to facilitate jumping clear of brush, downed logs and other common low-lying obstacles during flight from danger; perhaps to provide an elevated view of the surrounding terrain as the animal runs; perhaps to make it more difficult for pursuing predators to make physical contact; or perhaps as a signal to predators that they've been spotted and the stotting animal is healthy, fleet, and would prove to be a waste of time and energy to pursue.

Unlike whitetails, which, in areas of greatest concentration, sometimes "yard up" for the winter on a portion of the same relatively restricted, forested range they occupy in summer, mule deer are far-ranging and often travel several miles from their high-elevation summertime haunts down to more hospitable timbered valleys and sage flats for winter, where the snow cover is lighter and food is more abundant.

In the rugged mountains surrounding my home, for example, muleys are plentiful from late spring through early winter. But by the time the snow starts piling deep, usually before Christmas, they have all, or almost all, pulled out; only rarely will a deer track be seen hereabouts again until after Easter. But they don't go far; this annual departure isn't a real migration—just a little stroll of a few miles down the valley to where the wintertime pickin's aren't quite so slim.

It is on their wintering grounds that male deer, both mule and whitetail, drop off, or "cast," the previous year's racks and begin the almost magical process of antler regeneration. Come spring, a person who happens upon an abandoned deer wintering ground—as a friend of mine did just this past April over in the Utah sage flats—is likely to witness bleached antlers scattered like fallen limbs in an aspen forest. Unfortunately, the average observer will find it impossible to determine by what variety of deer the cast antlers he discovers were grown. But there are ways.

The definitive characteristic of whitetail antlers is that their tines, or points, sprout individually from the main beams, just as in elk. The first offshoot above the burr is a true brow tine (eye protector), notwithstanding its small size relative to the bez (second) and higher tines. The basal (bottom) portion of the main beam tends to be heavily "pearlated," having a knobby, beaded appearance.

As if intent on being distinct, a muley buck's antlers are dichotomous, or "bifurcate," with each main beam forking into two smaller beams and, in mature bucks, each of these two forking again for an average total of four tines per side, the exact number depending on age, health, nutritional status and genetic influences. In mule deer, basal pearlation can be extravagant, in extreme cases resembling melted wax dripped down the sides of a candle. There is some disagreement among biologists as to whether or not the relatively small "snag points" that sprout from just above the burrs of muley bucks are true brow tines—though the preponderance of expert opinion seems to agree they are, and they certainly look the part to me.

The good-old-boy system employed to report the number of tines a mule deer buck carries on his antlers is called, appropriately enough, "western count." It's unfortunate, though, that in western count the tines of only one side—typically the larger of the two, should they differ—are cited. Thus, a mule deer buck having three points on the right beam and four on the left would be a "four-pointer."

Whitetail antler points are reckoned differently, using a system known as "eastern count." I sometimes call this technique "braggart's count," since the tines on both antlers are tallied and totaled. Thus, a whitetail buck having three points on the right beam and four on the left would be a seven-pointer.

Neither of these popular systems, unfortunately, is really adequate for use by serious antler buffs. Eastern count indicates the total number of points but, in cases where that total is an odd number, fails to specify which beam has what. Meanwhile, western count provides an indication of the number of tines on only one beam and leaves to guesswork whether a "four-pointer" has four, three or some other number of tines on his other beam—or, for all we know, just the one antler. ("Unicorn" bucks, resulting from natural injuries, are not all that uncommon.)

There is, fortunately, a more precise way to count and report antler points. For lack of an official name, I call this system "elk count," since it's commonly used in scoring the antlers of that species. So far as I can figure, the only reason elk count hasn't yet been universally applied to whitetails, muleys and their subspecies everywhere is the stubborn tenacity of regional tradition—a situation analogous to trying to force Americans to switch from reckoning in pounds and feet to figuring in kilograms and meters.

With elk count, the number of right-beam tines is listed first, separated from the left by an "X." With this system, our hypothetical three-right, four-left rack would be reported as a 3 x 4, no matter the species. Elk count is slowly gaining favor among hunters and other antler fanciers, and eventually may overcome inertia to achieve popular sanction—though probably (and I would hope), under another name.

Three years have come and gone now since I sat mesmerized while that enigmatic doe and those three "one of a kind" mule deer bucks paraded across that high brushy ridgetop a few miles above my home. Although I've revisited that enchanted place many times since, early spring through late fall, I've encountered not a one of those big bucks again. Still, I dare to hope, and sometimes even trust, that all three, as well as the little doe, are yet alive, that the bucks have grown even larger, even more magnificent, and that the enigmatic doe has given birth to several new members of the local deer community.

# II

# THE ELUSIVE WAPITI
## *High, Wide and Handsome*

The moose is larger, the bear more powerful, the
mountain lion more mysterious and the whitetail
more graceful, but the bull wapiti, with his proud
posture, bugled call to arms and rich, tricolored
pelage is certainly the most regal of North America's
great wild creatures. And his crowning glory is a
magnificent rack of antlers.

—from *Among the Elk*

FREQUENTLY IN MY BACKCOUNTRY treks, what I find does not
conform to what I seek. But no matter, no real matter at all, for
nature is never disappointing.

This evening I have come afield in search of—not something with antlers, as is most often the case, but a creature
that preys upon the antlered species: bear. I have met bears
here before—up this big wooded draw a ways; down below
a fern-fringed grotto where a trickle of sweet spring water
escapes its subterranean confines. From the grotto, the tiny
flow snakes a hundred yards down the draw before being
detained by a small natural depression. The result is a hot-
tub-sized pool of cool, clear refreshment. A mere few
dozen yards below the pool, the overflow is recaptured by
the thirsty earth.

I have seen little evidence over the years to indicate that
many humans besides myself know of this quiet, hidden
place. But the animals—they know it well. Since this is the
only reliable and secluded water source hereabouts, the

pool is visited regularly by deer and elk and bears and birds and small creatures enough to fill an Audubon field guide.

But it's bear I've come here in hopes of seeing on this warm August evening. I have no fear of *Ursus americanus,* having found myself within breath-holding distance of the normally shy creatures on several occasions without getting mauled, chased, treed or in any other way molested. So far.

One of my more memorable bear encounters unfolded right here in this little draw, almost exactly three years ago. That evening, as it happened, I had come in search of elk. While standing motionless, inhaling the rich, fecund, fungal smell of this jungly place, I suddenly sensed—that is to say, my ears told me—that I was no longer alone. Opening my eyes, I found myself in the path of three badger-sized, dark-chocolate bear cubs. Here they came, sniffling and whimpering from out of the brush, and soon were playing at my very feet. One of them actually touched its curious nose to my leather boot.

The mother bear, a smallish sow with a chocolate back collared around with a swatch of blonde (I am yet to see a black "black bear" in these parts), appeared a minute later a couple of dozen yards up the draw and, fortunately for us all, up the downslope breeze. Grunting and rooting, she fed slowly down toward us.

I got a good long look at the sow before she breezed insouciantly by, headed down the draw. It was only with reluctance that the cubs abandoned their newfound upright curiosity and tagged along after her. Good thing they did, for no sooner had the sow disappeared from my view than she cut my scent trail. With an alarmed bawl she led her young helter-skelter out of harm's way and off into the forest gloaming.

The entire encounter had lasted perhaps five minutes. During that time I was keenly alert, at moments apprehensive, but my overflowing excitement, joy and sense of wonder held any real fear, or at least the recognition of it, at bay.

It was only later, after the excitement of the moment had passed, that I allowed myself to reflect on the documented fact that black bear attacks, while an insignificant threat in the big picture, nonetheless have resulted in scores of maulings and at least twenty-three deaths in North America in this century alone. Further, most of the attacking bears have been sows with cubs. That little chocolate-blonde bruin had, at one point, been within a two-second dash of me. Had she seen, smelled or otherwise sensed my human form standing like a statue in the midst of her cubs, there almost certainly would have been trouble.

On another occasion in another place, I was creeping through an aspen grove at the edge of a large alpine meadow, hoping to spot elk bedding along the opposite side, when my peripheral vision sensed movement a little farther into the timber, perhaps a dozen feet to my left. I stopped and turned and saw . . . the largest black bear I've ever encountered. The huge cinnamon-phase boar (few black bears in the Rockies are actually black, with cinnamon, brown and blonde phases far more plentiful) was walking along a downed log, apparently just for the sheer hell of it, just as I did frequently as a youngster and do yet today on capricious occasion.

The bear had apparently angled down off the slope to my left, through the thick aspen and conifer woods, and walked up behind me before passing close on my left. Given the black's reputation for wariness, I couldn't believe my fortune at having such a close encounter of the furred kind. Had I not been dressed in camo, had I been moving noticeably, or had the wind direction been different, I would never have seen that bear. Again, an awareness of potential danger came over me only after the fact.

So, while I do not fear black bears, and in fact always look forward to my next unscheduled meeting with them—that is, after all, why I have come to this very beary place this evening—I nonetheless grant them deferential courtesy.

Just now, I am standing quietly in the great white heart of the same parklike grove of quaking aspens where I met the four bears, but somewhat lower, down near the wide mouth of the draw. As always when I'm seriously searching for wildlife, I am scrubbed clean and as odorless as I can make myself, dressed cap-to-boots in camouflage, my face and hands painted with smears of green and black makeup. A camouflaged fanny pack girds my waist, and around my neck hang a pair of mini-binoculars.

I move slowly on, investing far more time in watching, listening, sniffing the air for familiar wild odors, than in walking. When I do move, it's easy does it: step quietly, carefully, then stop to look and listen, trying my best to be a proficient predator. But even with maximum concentration and effort, I lose this timeless game of cat-and-mouse far more often than I win, found out by the keen senses of my quarry—which either flee in a rustle of dry leaves, or remain still as death until I have bumbled past . . . and then flee in a rustle of dry leaves.

But on those priceless occasions when I do win—and they come somewhat more often than rarely—my reward is rich: the privilege to observe, hear, even smell, up close and relaxed, some of nature's most elusive wild creatures. These are the times that gladden my soul.

Satisfied that nothing lurks immediately ahead or around me now, I slip on through the aspen grove and work carefully up a dim but familiar game trail that leads me winding through a pristine jungle of montane forest understory—alpine lady fern, common lady fern, giant cow parsnips, pine drops and other lush, living things whose names I have yet to learn. The going here is easy, almost soundless, but the foliage is so thick that I can see only a few yards in any direction.

After half an hour of this creeping and peeping, I'm confronted by the huge shaggy reclining corpse of a ponderosa pine, recently fallen dead-center across the game trail. Both its gnarly butt and its pointy head lie in crushed tangles of its own limbs, oak brush and wild rose thorn; it would be all but impossible to work around either end without making a disruptive racket and then having to thrash my way back along the far side to regain the trail. Instead, I decide to climb directly over the shoulder-high trunk.

I snap a few small branches in negotiating the hefty trunk, but keep my profile low and manage the crossing without sounding a general alarm. After pausing a couple of minutes to regain a sense of quiet, I ease on up the narrowing draw, following the game run as it bends to the left, toward the evening's goal.

The moment the spring pool comes into sight, I glimpse movement on its far, or upper side. Whatever it is, it looks big. And in this verdant pocket of public domain, it has to be wild; the nearest cow or horse is miles away.

I freeze where I stand, fearful even to reach for my binoculars. Unaided, my eyes strain to identify this mysterious creature thrashing around in a tangle of chokecherry and aspen saplings less than fifty yards ahead. Up this far, the draw is deep, steep and so heavily wooded as to be in shadow even at midday, and it's now approaching sunset. All I can make out is a large, dark-brown head. A bear. It must be a bear. And a good big one at that. With this realization I am treated to a shot of adrenaline—a true "natural high" carrying no legal or moral penalty. I consider my next move: Forward, back or neither?

Looking again, I note that the mysterious head seems awfully long and narrow to belong to a bear. When it dips low, I make a slow reach for the binoculars riding at my chest, raise them to my eyes, focus.

Well. What we have here is no bear after all, but the elusive wapiti. A bull elk. When his head comes up and his antlers come momentarily into view, I count five, looks like maybe six tines to the side. High, wide and handsome, as befits this grand species. His big dark nose is pointed straight at me, but the eyes are showing white, rolled back, not looking, not seeing. He is distracted, lost in the rutting ritual of honing his antlers on a hapless sapling.

I watch this familiar action, now magnified seven-fold by optical magic, for a full minute. When the big brown head finally goes down again, I take one long, slow step to the side, off the open trail, and sink carefully to my knees. My camouflaged form dissolves into the forest understory. Or at least I hope it does.

Apparently finished for the moment with polishing his rack, the bull grows still and peers around, then turns and moves diagonally away from the spring pool, passing just thirty yards to my left. I wait a long minute, then stand and begin a careful advance.

At the lower edge of the pool, I stop to listen. I can still hear the animal banging about, but he sounds to be moving away rapidly; faster, I'm sure, than I can hope to follow in anything approaching silence.

Inspecting the pool, I note that the water, normally clear, is agitated and milky; its surface, normally a mirror for the trembling aspen leaves and sky above, is shimmering; its bottom, normally as smooth as the sand of a low-tide beach, is pocked with the bull's big post-hole prints. The aspen sapling he was bullying is totally denuded of bark from two to six feet above the ground. The air—the very atmosphere of this place—is charged with the funky barnyard stench of bull elk in rut.

I consider my next move, then slip into a poolside thicket of aspens, berry brush and ferns. A natural blind. Seated in relative comfort on a fallen log, I unbuckle my fanny pack and fish out a small, flat, half-moon disc of nylon and neoprene. A diaphragm elk call; one of the little "emergency" items I tote along on all my frequent forays into the local woods. This, clearly, is an emergency.

Being not quite late August, the elk rut is only just coming on; I have yet to hear the season's first bugle. Still, bugling would seem to be my only option. I can't trail the departing bull at a pace fast enough to keep up and not give myself away. If I want to win a better look at him, to feel the excitement of his nearby presence my only chance is to try and lure him back here. I place the call against the roof of my mouth, clamp it there with my tongue, take a deep breath, and exhale. Air screams out between tongue and palate, frantically vibrating the neoprene reed sandwiched in between—*Unnhh-eeeee-ungh!*

Even before the would-be bugle is complete, I sense that something is terribly amiss. The sound is sour, abrupt, discordant. Just plain wrong. I disgorge and examine the call, but can find no blameful flaw. No matter, for the nearby bull coughs—once, twice. A reply of sorts. He is apparently more curious than cautious.

I bugle again. It sounds a little better coming out this time, so I add a series of sharp braying coughs at the end—a boastful challenge.

My eight-hundred-pound adversary coughs twice more, stamps the ground, bangs his antlers against a tree. Silence, then the sound of heavy steps. The bull is coming.

The elusive bull elk, or wapiti: No other animal of the southern Rockies (now that the grizzly is all but locally extinct) excites, intrigues, fascinates and frustrates me nearly so thoroughly as he.

Part of my intense interest in this animal is a simple matter of supply and demand. While North America presently boasts a population of some seventeen to twenty-one million deer, we can claim only three-quarters of one million elk. That's a deer-to-elk ratio of roughly twenty-four to one. Moreover, the great bulk of that relatively small elk population is found in wild and self-sustaining numbers in just nine mountainous western states and the two westernmost Canadian provinces.

Although restricted in the continental view, the elk's stamping grounds nonetheless comprise some of the biggest, wildest, most exciting and least-spoiled country left anywhere in the temperate world. This good taste in habitat is yet another of the wapiti's special attractions. Elk are the native cutthroat trout of the mammalian world. Rarely will you find these sensitive creatures, these barometers of environmental quality, living wild and well amidst any but the most scenic and invigorating landscapes.

Then there's the eerie bugling of the bulls—a taut, stretched, flutelike sound unique in all of nature. A basic, or "challenge" bugle typically begins with a low, throaty growl, rises in scale to a siren's wail, continues its climb to plateau with a sustained whistle, then slides back down the octaves in a mirror image of its ascent. Often, a bull answering such a challenge will echo the challenger's bugle, then up the ante by capping his reply with a series of curt, braying coughs. As the action heats up, the opposing party may respond in kind, or forego the bugle altogether and shout back only the string of coughs. Ground-pawing, antler-banging, brush-busting and scent marking complete the act. Quite a show to hear, incredible to see, unforgettable to smell.

Along with the bugling of the autumn bulls, elk of both sexes make several other distinct sounds. These include the much quieter bugling of cows (most often heard in spring); loud, sharp, very doglike barks to register alarm; and a variety of calm, birdlike whistles and catlike mews uttered—primarily between cows and their calves—as "all's well" reports and to help a herd keep together in heavy cover.

In addition to the wapiti being the only member of the North American cervid community that produces sounds more complex than grunts, blatts, snorts and sneezes, the rutting bull elk's resonant, reverberating bugle is, I believe, one of the most enthralling sounds in the natural world. In North America today, only the haunting, joyful chorus of a wolf pack or coyote family, the rare defiant scream of a mountain lion or the ethereal evening calls of loons can come close to matching the bull elk's bugle for atavistic excitement and pure musical quality.

And the wapiti is big, outsized only by the moose. Mature bulls of most elk subspecies weigh close to eight hundred animate pounds (364 kilos), the size of a small horse. Females average a solid six hundred pounds (273k).

In spite of its great bulk, the wapiti is a past master of evasion. The seeker after wild elk, discounting dumb luck, has to *work* to find and close with this cagey beast. I specify "wild elk" because there is another variety . . . those semi-tame residents of western national parks and wildlife preserves that—a mixed blessing—can be easily approached, often to within a few foolish yards. I enjoy both, but, as with most things in life, I prefer the untamed and unspoiled.

Finally, even the animal's name is enchanting. *Wapiti* is an all-American word that originated on the pre-Columbian tongues of Shawnee Indians. It is generally interpreted to mean "white rump," in reference to the animal's large, light-colored (though actually more cream than white) butt patch. But the wapiti was roaming North America long before the arrival of the humans who first hung a name on it.

Notwithstanding its long residence here, the elk apparently did not evolve in North America. Its probable birthplace as a genus is Asia. In due time, some segments of that parent population wandered westward to occupy Europe. In this way, down through the millennia, Eurasia gained a variety of scattered but related elk species. The most abundant and best-known of these is the red deer—the stately "stag" praised in Old World poetry and prose since the very advent of written language. And probably earlier.

When conditions became favorable, Eurasian elk finally made the continental leap to North America. These crossings—plural, for no migration of any magnitude is a one-time event undertaken by a single group—took place over a long period of time during the gate-opening Illinoian and Wisconsin glacial stages, when growing ice masses "soaked up" a quantity of the northern seas sufficient to lower their levels and expose that well-trod isthmus long known as the Bering land bridge, more recently as Beringia.

Even today, elk on both sides of the now-sunken isthmus are considered by some leading researchers in both North America and Russia as—not only the same species, but the same *subspecies*. (Ditto for Siberian and American moose, and native East Siberian and Alaskan humans.) Those who adhere to this view dismiss differences in body size and antler mass and configuration as mere "temporary" responses to local quantity and quality of forage. To these taxonomic "lumpers" (more about which momentarily), the traits that really count in species determination—all genetic with a "high degree of expression": body-hair color, short tails, off-color rump patches, the presence of neck manes, vocalizations—are virtually identical on both sides of the slender Bering Strait.

In any event, from the moment of the elk's first landing in Alaska to the present, the animal has proven itself an adaptable and resilient pioneer. In time, descendants of the parent species drifted south and east, splitting and evolving into a variety of subspecies as they went. Eventually—given a generous lack of effective predators at the time—the genus became ubiquitous across most of temperate North America.

In pre-Columbian times, the elk was quite possibly the most widespread deer type in the Americas. At its peak, the species sprawled longitudinally from West Coast almost to East, and latitudinally from Canada on the north to the Mexican states of Durango and Hidalgo at the southern extreme of its range.

The Shawnee name *wapiti* is used interchangeably today with the term "elk," which is derived from *elch,* the German word for the animal known to North Americans as the moose. Thus, in Europe, our moose is called an elk, and our elk a red deer, or stag. It was to minimize just this sort of cross-language naming conflicts that Swedish biologist Carolus Linnaeus, way back in the eighteenth century, introduced a system for assigning to every living thing an internationally understood and honored scientific name. To avoid showing favoritism toward any living language (as has happened with German and the science of glacial geology), all scientific names are drawn from two classic but good and dead languages, Latin and ancient Greek.

Still, no system is without problems, and anyone who undertakes much prowling through the biological literature soon enough will be confronted with conflicting versions of the wapiti's proper scientific name. In older sources, the North American elk is referred to as *Cervus canadensis.* More recent texts call the same animal *Cervus elaphus*—the same species name as that worn by the wapiti's Eurasian conspecific, the red deer.

And from that curiosity hangs something of a tale.

In decades past, the tendency among biological taxonomists—those necessarily pedantic souls whose task it is to classify and assign scientific names to all living things—was to split a given genus into as many distinct species as existing knowledge suggested was supportable. Advocates of this "splitter" persuasion felt, and not without palpable evidence, that sufficient differences existed between red deer and wapiti—in body size and coloration, antler size and conformation, vocalizations, geographical location and other details—to designate each a separate species. Therefore, the red deer was tagged *Cervus elaphus*; the wapiti, *Cervus canadensis*.

More recently, however, the taxonomic tide has turned, with the opposing school of thought, the previously mentioned "lumpers," now dominating. Consequently, many once-split species are being reunited. Among those already lumped together are the European and American versions of the elk. And so it is, at least for the nonce, that the accepted scientific name for the wapiti is *Cervus elaphus*. Ten, twenty years from now—who can say?

(Late-breaking news: Here in Colorado, a law has just been passed that prohibits the import and keeping of certain "exotic" wild game species—including and especially the ranching of red deer, which is big business in New Zealand. Why the harsh proscription? Because state wildlife managers fear that some red deer might escape from their enclosures and breed with our native Rocky Mountain elk, thus "diluting the gene pool" and somehow making the wapiti less American.

Now, I ask you—if the red deer and the wapiti are classified as the same species, which they presently are, doesn't that suggest genetic identicality? And if, as Colorado wildlife managers obviously feel, there *is* a significant difference between red deer and elk, how can taxonomists continue lumping them together as conspecifics? Should this anti-red deer bias grow and spread to other western states, I suspect the splitters will once again float to the top.)

Biological taxonomy, like math and philosophy, is the sort of thing that if not fully understood can prove to be deadly boring. Once the scheme is locked onto, however, the scientific naming game can actually become fun. Sort of.

In that spirit—and operating under the assumption that, since you're reading this book, you may well be an amateur naturalist yourself (whether you've thought of your interest in nature that way before this moment or not) and eager to learn—I offer the following mercifully brief overview of the taxonomy of modern cervids. (For a complementary schematic of cervid taxonomy, see Appendix A.)

All North American deer belong to the kingdom Animalia (as opposed to Plantae, the plants), the phylum Chordata (the vertebrates plus some notochordate marine animals), the class Mammalia (endothermic, or warm-blooded animals that suckle their young), the order Artiodactyla (the even-toed ungulates), the suborder Ruminantia (the cud-chewers, having multi-compartmented stomachs) and the family Cervidae (the deer).

Within the Cervidae family there are four genera: caribou (*Rangifer*), moose (*Alces*), the deer proper (*Odocoileus*) and elk (*Cervus*). Each genus is further divided into a varying number of species, and the species into subspecies or races.

Fortunately, it's the custom, even among the most pedantic of scientists, to abbreviate this complex strata and identify animals by their most specific—that is, genus, species and sometimes subspecies—names only. Thus, the North American elk is known—not as Animalia Chordata Mammalia Artiodactyla Ruminantia Cervidae *Cervus elaphus subspecies*, but merely as *C. e. subspecies*. (As you may already have noted, when written, biological classifications above the level of genus are capitalized but not italicized, while genus is both capitalized and italicized, and species and subspecies designations are italicized but not capitalized. Don't ask me why.)

In North America, the species *C. elaphus* is further divided into four living subspecies (until quite recently there were six, but that's "progress"). The Rocky Mountain elk (*C. e. nelsoni*), known also as the Yellowstone elk, is the most plentiful and widespread North American wapiti race, ranging over virtually the entire north-south length of the Rockies. This is the elk of its namesake Yellowstone National Park as well as my Colorado stamping grounds and is, in my mind, the classic model, the elk of elks.

The Manitoban elk (*C. e. manitobensis*) is a stay-at-home Canuck inhabiting the Canadian provinces of Saskatchewan and Manitoba. This race is larger of body, smaller of antlers, darker in color and far less plentiful and widespread than the Rocky Mountain elk.

The Roosevelt's elk (*C. e. rooseveltii*), also called the Olympic elk, makes its home in the Pacific mountain forests of Oregon and Washington state, with smaller, transplanted populations inhabiting coastal islands off southwestern Canada and the Kodiak chain of Alaska. Heftier even than the Manitoban, the Roosevelt's is the largest-bodied of the four North American subspecies. Even so and oddly, its antlers typically are no match for those produced by the smaller-bodied Rocky Mountain race.

Last and in several ways least is the Tule elk (*C. e. nannodes*), also known variously as the California, valley and dwarf elk. This not only is the smallest-bodied and smallest-antlered of all the wapiti, but also the rarest. Just 2,500 of the "dwarf" animals (a bit of an overstatement considering that the bulls average 550 pounds/250 kilos, cows four hundred pounds/182k) exist today in pockets of protected habitat scattered across central and northern California. This is the species that obliged me with that fortuitous Big Sur roadside encounter . . . all those years ago, all those miles away.

The bull is coming. In answer to my challenging call, the big animal has hauled around and is returning to the spring pool near where I sit hidden.

My adrenaline buzz, so invigorating and welcome just minutes ago, has intensified to the point that it's beginning to rattle my composure, blur my vision, plunge my hands into spasms of palsy. I close my eyes, take a deep breath, hold, meter its slow exhalation.

Yes, the bull is coming, but slowly, tentatively; he's not exactly hot to trot. Not like some others I've called in. To warm him up, to fan the smoldering coals of his emerging rutting rage, I bugle again.

The bull's response is lukewarm, disappointing: a snort, the thud of a single hoof stamping the ground, a rattling of antlers in the brush. But no reply bugle. And though he is still coming and now in fact is but a rock's chuck away, he's staying behind the dense foliage above the pool. Maintaining good cover. Keeping himself in defilade. Offering my straining, hungry eyes no more than an occasional tidbit of grayish pelage, a few flashes of ivory-tipped antler.

As the bull continues his careful reconnoitering of my hiding place, I tumble at last to what he's up to: The scheming beast plans to sneak around me, down the slope, downwind and then across until he cuts my scent trail. He'll have me then.

And he does exactly that—circumambulating, maneuvering, soon enough inhaling what to him must be the fetid stench of my humanity. The bull registers his disgust with a bark—not a "barklike sound," but a sharp, very loud and doglike bark—an alarm as piercing as an air horn, as sure in its meaning as a slap in the face.

My game is bankrupt. Once again, the elusive wapiti has won. I am granted a final brief glimpse of hair and antler, the soft, going-away sound of a few careful hoof-falls as the gray ghost-king of this high mountain valley fades from flesh and bone reality into the nostalgic realm of fond memory.

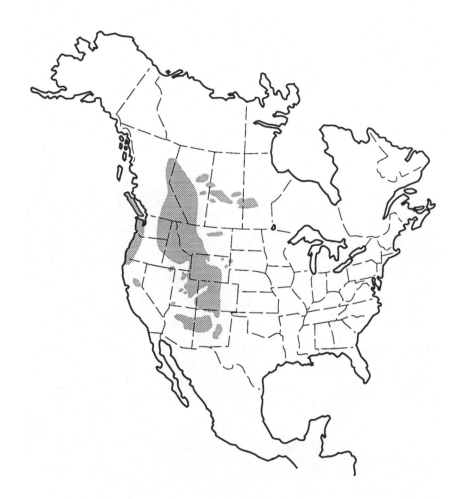

ELK DISTRIBUTION

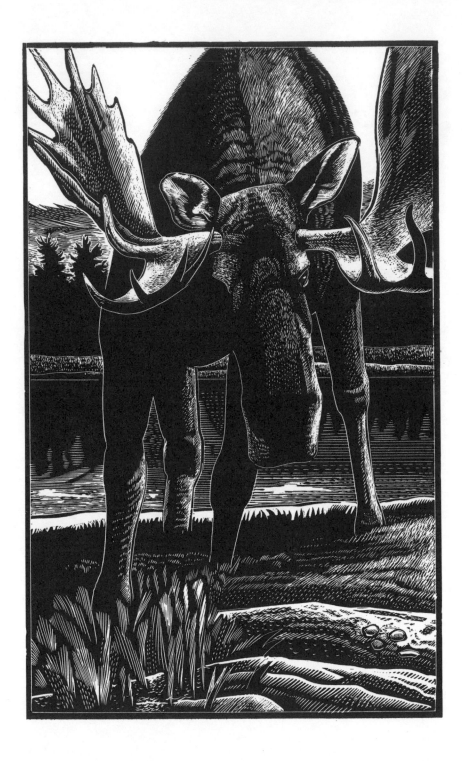

# ❧ III.

# CONSIDER THE COMELY MOOSE
## *No More Mr. Nice Guy*

> The [charging bull] Moose evidently had his eyes on
> Joe on account of his having had the lantern, and this
> gave me a good opportunity to find a tree for myself.
> I had just time to get clear when [the moose] arrived
> at the foot of my tree. . . . I told Joe we might as well
> make up our minds to stay there for the night. . . .
> The Moose stood guard until 2 A.M., when he left. . . .
> We waited about another hour, and came down, as
> it was getting daylight. We were pretty hungry for
> supper that morning I can assure you.
>
> —GEORGE GIBBONS
> in E.T. Seton's *Lives of Game Animals*

CONSIDER THE COMELY moose. While he is normally the most
sedate of North America's four deer species, he can, under the
right (or, as some people who have been there would say, the
*wrong*) circumstances, be a full ton of raging terror: No more
Mr. Nice Guy, indeed.

Of my own humble moose encounters, the most exciting,
thus far, was a short bluff charge by a young Shiras bull I
virtually stumbled over while hiking in Yellowstone country. I
came, I saw, I froze. He saw, he came (fast), I went.

My other moose encounters have all been mere sightings—
the largest Shiras bull I've ever seen, ambling down the
highway just east of Cooke City, Montana; a lone cow near
Crazy Creek, along the Clark's Fork of the Yellowstone River
in Montana, that stood dumbly, a snack of wildflowers

dangling yellow and green from her drooling mouth while a friend and I passed within a few yards on a nearby foot trail; a young bull that galloped across the highway in front of the same friend and me a few miles south of LaBarge, Wyoming, then leapt a five-strand barbed wire fence with the agility of a steeplechaser and stopped to see if we'd noted the feat; and, just this past September, in the Alaskan bush, a medium-sized Alaska-Yukon bull (and even at that, he was a great deal larger than my largest Shiras) that came down to the river near camp for a drink, scattering a flock of canvasbacks into panicked and cacophonous flight in the process, then disappeared back into the alders from which he had come.

Four North American moose subspecies are currently recognized for antler scoring by the Boone and Crockett and Pope and Young clubs: the Alaska-Yukon moose (*Alces alces gigas*), the Canada or Eastern moose (*A. a. americana*), the Northwestern or Anderson's moose (*A. a. andersoni*) and the Shiras or Wyoming moose (*A. a. shirasi*).

Standing some seven feet high at the shoulders and more than nine feet in length, the Alaska-Yukon moose is the largest member of the deer family living today—of a bodily size, in fact, with the extinct Irish elk, or a Belgian draft horse. You can't fully appreciate this beast's bulk until you've seen one up close in the wild or, at the least, gawked at the crowd-stopping specimen stuffed and standing lifelike in a towering glass case at Anchorage International Airport.

In addition to being the largest of body, the Alaska-Yukon moose also carries the heftiest "horns" of any living cervid. The greatest antler spread for its race, as listed in the Boone and Crockett Club's *Records of North American Big Game* (eighth edition), is 81.5 inches (two-plus meters), or nearly seven feet. How does an animal manage to grow—and cast, and regrow annually—such huge bony structures, year after year throughout its life?

In all deer species, the antler cycle (growth, maturity, social employment, casting) is inextricably tied to the annual mating season, or rut. Through natural selection, cervids have evolved a mechanism by which all mature and healthy male deer of all genera, species and subspecies will be equipped with fully developed and hardened antlers just when they're needed most.

The timing of the rut—which varies significantly by species and to a lesser extent by latitude—in its turn, is controlled by hormone secretions triggered in the hypothalamus. Pulling this chemical trigger is photoperiod, the seasonally varying number of daylight hours, as measured by the retinas of the eyes. And cocking the hypothalamus's hammer, so to speak, is length of gestation. Large deer types, such as moose and elk, must carry their unborn young longer than relatively small species, such as the whitetail. Since weather and food availability fairly dictate that the young of all deer species be born in late spring, the larger-bodied varieties must rut earlier.

As we have seen, antlers sprout from pedicles—those two short, permanent projections of living, skin- and hair-covered bone that jut from the foreheads of all North American species of male deer. (Pedicles have the *genetic potential* to appear in female cervids as well, but their development, except in caribou, is held in check by the presence of female hormones and the absence of testosterone.) While pedicle development in male moose begins soon after birth, actual antler growth doesn't commence until the following spring.

A young bull moose's first set of antlers typically are short, single-beamed, unpalmate "spikes." Occasionally, simple forks crown their tips. The second cycle's growth is larger, with the main beams distinctly forked and the beginnings of palmation evident. Overall size continues to increase for several years thereafter, with maximum antler growth being attained between the ages of seven and ten. Beyond this age, gradual atrophy sets in, rendering older, postprime bulls less successful in the annual mating competition.

Until shortly before time for a pair of antlers to be dropped, or "cast"—for moose, this generally takes place in December—the antler-pedicle connection will remain so firm that you could literally swing from the antlers without fear of breaking them loose and falling. Then, within the span of just a few days, testosterone levels drop sharply, prompting the bone tissue connecting antlers and pedicles to erode, dissolve and be resorbed into the body. In effect, the "glue" that binds antlers to pedicles dissolves and is carried away by the bloodstream.

After antler casting, the newly exposed pedicle tops are left raw and bloody, looking not unlike the ends of freshly cut-through living bone. But scabs soon form and pre-velvet skin begins migrating in from the outer edges of the wound, providing protection for the underlying development of new antler buds.

The cells responsible for the elongation of growing antlers, called osteoblasts, are among the fastest-multiplying of any mammalian tissue—faster, even, than cancer cells—requiring, on the average, only 150 days to equip a healthy, mature, well-fed bull moose with its incredibly heavy rack of antlers. In one of cervid authority Valerius Geist's studies, the antler weights of 140 trophy-class Alaska-Yukon bulls averaged just under fifty-one pounds (23.2 kilos), with the heaviest going nearly eighty pounds (36.2k). In the latter case, that translates to an average growth rate of more than a third of a pound per day.

Antlers grow not from their bases, as do horns, but elongate at the tips of the main beams and tines by way of cartilage deposition. This special antler-growth cartilage is produced by the aforementioned osteoblasts, which do most of their work between the antler and its skinlike velvet covering. But unlike cartilage found elsewhere in the body, the type involved in antler growth is honeycombed with vertical columns of blood vessels.

The primary blood suppliers for growing antlers are the superficial temporal arteries that run up the sides of the head to feed a dozen or so smaller, branching arteries delivering oxygenated blood to the pedicles. Vessels sandwiched between the velvet and the antlers transport the blood up to the growing tips, from where the essential fluid percolates down through vessels located deep within the growing antlers' cores and out to their velvet-covered surfaces. A glance at a pair of dry, "finished" antlers, especially those of moose and other palmated species, will reveal the deep meandering grooves of these former superficial (surface) arterial channels.

While new cartilage is forming at the growing antler tips, older cartilage farther down the shafts is being replaced by a soft, fibrous bone matrix that rises from the pedicles. As growth progresses, the invading bone matrix gradually "ossifies," or hardens, in a process known as mineralization.

Like so: Toward the end of the growth period, after spongy bone matrix has completely replaced cartilage, calcium and phosphorus extracted from mineral-rich foods (young willow is a primary source for moose) and deposited in the skeleton are withdrawn and transported by the bloodstream to the growing antlers. To accomplish this feat of mineral trans-ference, rather than banking up large reserves of minerals prior to antler growth, the skeleton apparently just speeds up its mineral uptake-and-release process.

An interesting and relevant side note drawn from conversa-tion with Dr. Jerrett Newbrey, of Washington State University's Department of Veterinary and Comparative Medicine: In his extensive antler-growth research with reindeer (the caribou's domesticated Eurasian cousin), Newbrey has found that mineral drain from the skeleton to the forming antlers is so severe in many, if not most cases, that male cervids—not just reindeer, but all deer species—actually become osteoporotic. That is to say, the large bones of male cervids' skeletons give up so much of their mineral content during the peak of the annual antler-growth cycle that they become decalcified and brittle. The fact that the animals are capable of healing them-selves so very rapidly after completion of antler growth is one of the great miracles of nature. And just *how* they are able to do this, on an annual basis and without suffering any lingering ill effects, remains one of nature's greatest mysteries.

Be that as it may, upon reaching the antlers, calcium and phosphorus infiltrate the pores of the spongy matrix where they solidify, creating mature antler that is nothing more or less than solid (marrowless), dead bone.

By late August, with the rut rapidly approaching and the velvet's work done, testosterone levels increase, prompting the shut-off of blood flowing to the antlers. Robbed of its nourishment, the velvet soon begins to dry and split, peeling away from the antlers in long bloody shreds. This shedding of the velvet apparently is a somewhat irritating process, for the males of all deer species hasten it along by scraping their antlers against brush and trees. In this way, the velvet is shed—start to finish—generally within a day or two.

As the rut progresses, the antler-rubbing process that began during the velvet-shedding phase increases in fury, with moose bulls (in fact, the males of all cervid species) vigorously "horning" a variety of inanimate objects—trees, brush, the ground. While males of the deer family also rub trees and brush to spread pheromones emitted by the pre-orbital glands a good bit if not most horning seems to take place for no reason other than to exercise the fresh antlers. This rubbing action coats the new, raw, blood-stained rack with a variety of plant enzymes that react with oxygen and chemicals contained in the bloodstains to form a dark patina. Except at the tips of the tines. Here, the antler is less porous and thus, less absorbent.

By early September, the new antlers are finished and ready for action.

It might seem that the broad, flat antlers of a bull moose would make lousy weapons—unlike the spiky headgear of deer and elk. They are, in fact, more defensive than offensive in design, the massive palms—the Boone and Crockett record is fifty-six inches long by thirty wide (1.4 meters by seventy-six centimeters)—serving as heavy shields to deflect the jabs of opponents. Still, the numerous long, sharp tines projecting from the main antler beams and palms of a prime bull moose can be deadly when bulldozed into a rival's vitals. (Surprisingly, bull moose and the males of other deer species typically use their antlers as weapons only against one another; the primary weapons of defense against predators—and, on rare occasion, interloping humans—are flailing front hooves.)   .

Rutting battles and the behavior associated with them are highly ritualized. When one bull moose challenges another for the company of a cow, the challenger will strut up to the defender in a confident manner, rocking and dipping his head to offer the most fearsome view of his rack. Next come threatening bluff maneuvers that may include grunting, stamping the ground and vigorous horning of trees and brush.

While the challenger is carrying on in this haughty manner, the defender may retreat briefly to his cow (bull moose rarely gather harems, but rather visit estrous cows serially), perhaps to check her reaction—positive or negative?—to the intruder. Either way, his determination appears to gain strength and he soon returns to the fray to toss off some threats of his own, trying to one-up his challenger.

If one or the other bull can—via antler displays, aggressive vocalizations and threatening body gestures—convince the other that he is the indisputable king of that particular mountain, the intimidated party will stomp off a ways, stop, and begin to feed or in some other fashion pretend nonchalance. The king, meanwhile, will indulge in such victory celebrations as wallowing and horning, all the while keeping a covert eye out for a surprise counterattack by the invariably sore loser. In this way, through show and bluff, many if not most dominance contests are settled without recourse to physical violence.

This makes good evolutionary sense, given that it would work against both the physical and the procreational good of the individual—and, so it must follow, the species—for prime breeding males to annually and actively attempt to mutilate and kill one another. It is for this very reason that conflicts between rutting males of most cervid species have evolved to be more ceremonial than physical. Which is not to say that serious, life-threatening battles between rutting males don't take place; they do in all deer species, and are especially prevalent among moose. Valerius Geist's extensive field studies in Canada have shown that mature moose bulls, even given their complex avoidance rituals, commonly receive from thirty to fifty puncture wounds *each year.* And combat deaths do occur. The point being: Without avoidance rituals, the carnage would be far greater.

In those instances when the ceremonials fail and a fight is to be, it typically will open with a shoving match, the goal being to put your opponent off balance and then seize the advantage to gore him in the ribs or another vital area (the venerated "kick 'em while they're down" school of close combat). Once in a great while (in two to five percent of all battles), one bull will kill another outright. And on rare occasion, two battling bulls will become antler-locked; if they can't work free, both may die from exhaustion, dehydration or starvation, or fall easy prey to predators.

After the rut, the importance of antlers diminishes sharply, though neighboring bull moose continue to spar in order to maintain their established social ranking. Although technically dead from shortly after the time the velvet is shed, the antlers continue to dry and become ever more brittle as they age. In due time, answering to the season's declining hours of daylight and a resulting drop in testosterone levels in the blood, the bond between antlers and pedicles deteriorates, as we have seen, and the heavy appendages drop off.

❧

Perhaps it's all those hormones bouncing around, together with the physical strain involved in growing and employing such monstrous racks in sparring contests and outright battles, that can sometimes turn a normally sedate bull moose into a love-blinded Jekyll and Hyde monster. (Remember the Maine bull moose that recently won national news headlines for romancing a barnyard cow?) In addition to chasing wayward pedestrians up trees, bull moose in rut have frequently been known to pursue people on horseback— though whether the intent was to tromp the rider or to court the horse (or vice versa) remains open to argument. Either way, the effect is always pretty much the same for rider *and* mount: surprise and sincere, justifiable terror.

The normally easy-going, almost slothful moose— dangerous? Well, one wisened old Montana hunting guide once commented, in all seriousness, that he'd take his chances with a grizzly bear over a rutting bull moose any day. The grizzly, he opined, is at least *somewhat* predictable, but a love-sick bull moose—especially he who is yet to be loved in return—is easily as edgy and potentially as dangerous as— well, as the male human animal under similar circumstances.

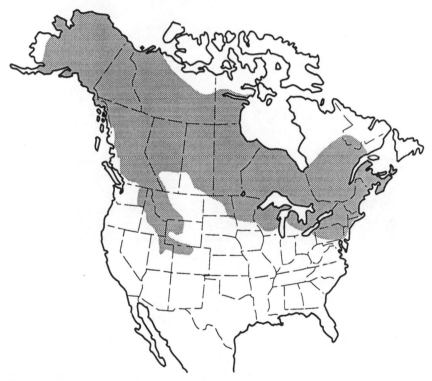

**MOOSE DISTRIBUTION**

# IN THE LAND OF THE CARIBOU
## *Pleistocene Dreaming*

The Reindeer [caribou] has always been an
important animal to our race. The dawn of human
history is known as "The Reindeer Age," because, at
that time, the Reindeer was the most numerous large
animal in Europe, and the chief support of man.

—ERNEST THOMPSON SETON
from *Lives of Game Animals*

AUTUMN, THAT BRIGHTEST and briefest of seasons.

A remote bush camp along a big slow bend of a major
tributary of Alaska's mighty Mulchatna River.

My good friend Bruce Woods and I arrived here yesterday,
gliding in by float plane. When the little craft lifted, dripping
diamonds of river water from its bulbous floats, and disappeared over the low hills, I was confronted with a certain hard
reality, more exciting than worrisome, but a fact nonetheless:
We were, and are, some three hundred air miles from
Anchorage and more than a hundred from our bush pilot's
home base, the native fishing village of Iliamna, itself quite
remote. To walk out across the rolling, roadless expanses of
sodden tundra framing the horizon all around would be a
physical impossibility. Even if we knew the way. Which we
don't. We will be here for nine days. We are happy.

After settling in, we dug out our fishing rods and angled the
evening away.

This morning it is cold, gray, windy, the air charged with
winter pending. We knock down a quick breakfast, pull on hip

waders, load our packs with a day's provisions and strike out across the tundra in search of the barren ground caribou that make this raw landscape their home—they are, in fact, the reason we have traveled all the very long way to be here. Although we spotted several dozen of the big deer during our low flight in yesterday, along with a few moose and one huge, glossy black bear, we are yet to get a good, long, ground-level look at a mature caribou bull. This is what we hope to accomplish today.

We top out on the low hills flanking the river, stop to look back from whence we just came, then walk on.

"Walking" is rather a casual term for the way a body gets around on foot in this country. At the best of times, you can in fact merely walk. More often, most often, you're slogging or sloshing: slogging across damp, spongy, foot-deep masses of lichens and mosses—tundra—or sloshing through knee-deep (and deeper) marshes. Thus the hip waders.

But the toughest going of all is over, around and through the sedge tussocks: tough, foot-high, grassy clumps that are broad across their tops and narrow at their bases, like giant mushrooms. Where patches of these little beauties occur, spanning usually an acre or more in extent, the individual clumps are too close together to step between, while walking over them is next to impossible, their rounded tops bending and rolling under your weight. If the sedge tussocks don't twist your ankles, they'll wrench your knees. At best, they'll leave you sore-boned and dog tired.

Caribou probably don't mind the tussocks so much, tip-toeing on hooves little larger than the heel of a man's hunting boot. Remarkably, these selfsame hooves also allow caribou to walk and run with ease across spongy tundra and even through boggy marshes—marshes into which a man, even given his much lighter weight supported by much larger feet, might sink knee-deep (as I have verified already during the brief course of this morning's trek).

The caribou's remarkable all-terrain mobility is possible because natural selection has equipped the animal with expansible hooves. On solid ground, the hooves are sized and shaped pretty much as you might expect for an animal of the caribou's bulk and weight—much larger than those of deer and smaller than those of elk. But unlike any other cervid, let a caribou trod upon something soft, and the hooves flare radically, the two sides, or "toes," spreading so wide that the tracks imprint almost perfectly round, sometimes appearing to be even broader than they are long.

Further, milleniums of migrating across and adapting to tundra and deep snow have provided caribou with outsized dewclaws (more accurately, dewhooves). This pair of atrophied, vestigial hooves, dangling just above the hooves proper, flare out when they make contact with soft ground, providing yet more surface area and giving caribou the greatest hoof-size to body-weight ratio of any cervid.

Likewise, in the water—which is everywhere here in this marshy land of the caribou—the animal's versatile hooves, splayed open to serve as paddles, make it the strongest, fastest and most confident swimmer of the deer family.

The wind in this largely treeless country blows incessantly and even now, in late September, carries on its back an arctic chill. After a couple of hours of walking, slogging and sloshing along, having seen no living creature larger than a raven, Bruce and I drop our packs and hunker down on the leeward side of a low hill, close against a sheltering clump of dwarf spruce.

From this comfortable vantage, we let our binoculars do the walking while we lie low—out of the wind, cheered by clearing skies, basking beneath a warming sun. As a bonus, without even sitting up I can reach around me and paw in fistfuls of ripe blueberries, bigger and sweeter than any I've ever known in the lower forty-eight, wild or domestic. I stuff these into my face until lips, tongue, fingers are stained dark.

I groan, feeling not unlike a berry-bloated bear.

If I *were* a local bear, I muse, I reckon I'd be right here on this very hill, lolling under this very sun, doing the very thing I'm doing right now—stuffing my furry face with blueberries.

Of course, being right here on this particular berry-rich knob of a hill wouldn't be necessary to make for a content ursine existence, since low-bush berries—blues, rasps, crans, crows, clouds (the natives call them salmonberries), currants, others I can't put a name to—are ubiquitous across the Alaskan tundra. Out here, the concept of a berry "patch" seems piddling.

And then there are the caribou; given the lack of wolves in this area, the bears have the caribou—or at least those relative few among the vast herds that are sick, lame, lazy, aged, very stupid, very young or otherwise easily catchable—all to themselves.

Bruce, binoculars seemingly glued to his eyes, is on wildlife watch, so I feel free to continue my loose-jointed reverie, rolling over on my berry-bloated belly for a close-up look at the spongy palatte of greens, yellows, golds and sands that paints this strange barren landscape to which the long-ago Lapps gave the name *tundar*.

From a distance, the low-lying, compact, multi-colored conglomeration of life that floors the tundra puts me in mind of the semi-arid prairies of the intermountain West. Upon this canvas, caribou—a small group of which Bruce has just spotted, half a dozen soft white dots floating in the far distance—remind me of pronghorn "antelope" in pronghorn country; out on the rolling prairies of central Wyoming, say. But while the pronghorn has adapted to its open habitat by developing uncanny distance vision, the caribou, oddly, has done no such thing. Knowing this, we gather up our gear, abandon our bright warm vantage and scurry, fully exposed, downslope toward them.

As we draw nearer, our binoculars show us that the little herd contains not six, but seven animals: three mature cows, three adolescent males and a tree-antlered herd bull. We're not quite close enough to make out the finer details of the big bull's headgear; still, his long, white mane sets him apart from the others and tells us that here is something special.

We move on toward the caribou, being more cautious now. They aid us by holding to their course, feeding generally in our direction. In less than an hour, with the unknowing cooperation of our quary, we close the gap from perhaps two miles to less than a quarter of one.

But now the animals stop, mill around for a few minutes, then lie down for a siesta. No way of knowing how long they'll stay down, and we've already crept to the last patch of dwarf spruce between us and them. There's nothing for it but to make ourselves comfortable, dig out our lunches and settle in for a possibly long spell of spying, while our seven subjects chew lazy cud and nap. For the best of the rest of the afternoon, that's exactly they way it goes.

On several occasions during this slow time, a cow or one of the smaller bulls rises and begins tentatively feeding, circling its companions, apparently in an attempt to get them up and moving. But so long as the big herd bull stays down, it seems, none of the others is going anyplace. Watching the old patriarch trying to nap out there in the open, under the bright warm Alaskan sun, prompts me to ponder something I've never before considered: How, I wonder, does a large male cervid deal with his antlers when he wants to sleep?

The old bull Bruce and I are watching stretches his head out flat in front of him, chin to the ground like a dog, and tries to keep his mountain of antlers balanced more or less vertically. But balancing that much weight and mass in your sleep can't be easy, and soon, sure enough, the big rack sags slowly to one side, crimping the animal's neck, bringing him awake.

Now the bull attempts to rest one main beam on the ground; to sleep with his head cocked to the side. But this technique proves even less satisfactory, leaving the poor fitful beast to shift constantly, searching for but never seeming quite to find that elusive comfort zone. Instead, he nibbles at sleep in what must be frustrating little bites.

Time passes effortlessly in this timeless land. Taking advantage of this lengthy lull in the action to resume my interrupted daydreaming, I gaze around me and reflect that this lean country has changed very little, if at all, since the late Pleistocene. It's entirely possible, even probable, that more than once in the past few thousand years stone-age hunters have squatted here on this very vista. Looking around them, they would have seen virtually the exact scenery Bruce and I are enjoying now.

Including the caribou.

Especially the caribou, for this abundant and not overly skittish animal would have been a meaty mainstay of their hunting, gathering and fishing economy. I smile to myself: To hell with "one giant step for mankind." I prefer the old, the simple, the sustainable. Eden was the hunting-gathering way of life, Eve's bite from the forbidden fruit a metaphor for man's transition to an agriculture-based economy . . . the original sin that led to fat times, a geometrically increasing human population, disease, famine, starvation, government and politics. Just look where it's got us.

Bruce gives my shoulder a good shake, rousing me from my Pleistocene daydreaming.

"Dave," he says, "they're getting up."

Finally, some three hours after the seven animals bedded, the burly boss has come to his feet. After gawking about for a long moment, much as I do after an afternoon nap, the old bull shakes his long mane, then ambles over to the larger of the three younger males—the second in command, as it were—and prods him in the ribs with a palmate antler tip. *El segundo* rises quickly at this rude prompting, shies away from his tormentor, then strolls over to the next smaller bull, upon whom he inflicts an equally pointed wake-up. Now, the fourth and smallest bull and all three cows clamber to their feet, evidently anxious to spare themselves similar rude treatment.

For the next few minutes, the animals mill around, feed half-heartedly, or merely stand there, appearing groggy from their long rest. But the October rut is rapidly approaching, and the hormones must already be working down deep in the bellies of the males, for the big bull now starts running *El segundo* in circles, attempting, it seems, to initiate a sparring contest. But of such lopsided sport the significantly smaller bull will have none, trotting out of harm's way while keeping a wary eye on the champ. The big bull makes threatening gestures with his antlers, but doesn't give further chase.

For the nonce, this is mere game-playing. But come the leading edge of the rut, in a couple of weeks or so, the big bull will drive these three young would-be studs away and set about gathering in more cows—up to a dozen or so if he's lucky. Or if he's good.

Again following the lead of the herd bull, the second bull wanders back to the group and starts hazing the third, and, lo and behold, the third bull a few moments later gives the same treatment to the fourth and lowest male on the totem pole. Through all of this, the three cows remain insouciant, grazing quietly, apparently undisturbed by all this macho bluff and nonsense.

The male pecking order thus reconfirmed, the animals begin actively feeding, drifting toward a small creek a few dozen yards to their front, its steep banks bearded with a low brushy growth of alder and willow.

With the caribou's movements putting some natural cover between us and them, Bruce and I finally may be able to sneak closer. We rise and move out.

After backtracking and circling downwind, dodging around a broad marsh in the process, we enter the brush along the creek and creep toward the feeding animals. But caribou can graze faster than most humans can run, much less sneak, and it takes us nearly an hour of strenuous physical activity to close the distance to under a hundred yards. Now the real stalk begins.

Using the same caution we've employed in past outings when attempting to approach elk or deer, Bruce and I bend low and painfully inch to within what we reckon to be twenty yards or less of the big bull, who sounds to be thrashing around just ahead in the alders. We can't see him, but our ears tell us that he is near and, judging from the racket, is either massacring all three of the smaller bulls, engaged in an orgy with the cows or clear-cutting a landing strip in the brush. Suddenly the commotion ceases. Is he on to us? Sensing we can sneak no closer, we ease up out of the creek bed, boldly revealing ourselves, hoping for a good, if brief, close look.

His antlers are more than impressive: Broad, tall, the color of fine mahogany, the beds of former sub-velvet arteries meandering like prairie creeks across the smooth-polished surfaces. The wrist-thick main beams arc back, up and forward, their tips palmed out as wide as a blacksmith's hands and each fingered with half a dozen big upthrusting points. The bez, or second tines, also widely palmated at their tips, reach forward then curve in, like a man's arms encircling the waist of an invisible sweetheart. The left brow tine is enlarged and flattened into a broad vertical "shovel" that extends out over the muzzle.

That this old fellow has recently been making good use of his impressive headgear is obvious from the condition of the foliage roundabouts—thumb-thick alder and willow brush slashed, crushed, split, peeled, bent, broken. The rampage responsible for this wholesale destruction no doubt was the source of the commotion we were hearing while creeping toward the bull: A prime male preparing himself for the approaching rut. Not only does such brush-busting help to relieve a pre-rut bull's pressurized libido, it also serves to polish his proud rack, strengthen his neck and develop a keenly honed kinesthetic sense of the size and exact shape of his antlers—a true sixth sense essential to victory, sometimes even to survival, in rutting combat.

The bulls senses us and flees—but not before we've had a chance to study and admire every feature of this grand creation of time and competition. Not just the antlers, but the big blunt nose capping the end of a broad, brown muzzle. The huge dark eyes framed by circles of short light hair. The flowing white neck mane. The rich chocolate pelage of the back. The white rump patch and undertail (no other cervid has so beautiful a cloak as the barren ground 'bou). The expansible hooves and big dangling dewclaws.

Already, on the first full day afield, we have found what we came here for.

It has been a full and rewarding day out here on the Alaskan tundra. We have worked long and hard to get close to a fine bull and, in the doing, have learned a little something, through first-hand observation, of the daily routines and social interactions of caribou in the wild.

But now, well into the lingering Alaskan twilight, we realize suddenly that the day's most lasting memory is yet to be made. Is being made—for a grizzly bear has just appeared, standing skylined less than a hundred yards up the hill from us. Downwind; he, or she, definitely knows we're here. It is a barren ground grizzly, as opposed to the larger coastal brown bear. Even so, it is the biggest, most fearsome, most beautiful animal I have ever seen. Standing up there now, its fur glowing softly under the waning sun, the creature seems surreal. A dream straight out of the Pleistocene. A dream that could quickly become a nightmare.

The grizzly pauses, tasting the breeze with muzzle elevated, obviously intrigued, though apparently not the least bit intimidated, by the stench of man sweat. Now it drops its massive head and comes—not straight on, but angling toward us, pausing and posing, being polite, clearly telling us that it is high time we went.

We are easily, almost instantly persuaded—a grizzly that shows no fear of man is a bear to be avoided. We make rapid preparations to leave, snatching up our packs and pulling them quickly onto our shoulders. By the time we begin our retreat—three minutes at the outside from the time we first spotted the interloper (or are *we* the interlopers?)—the bear is very close. Too close. Bringing up the rear, I glance frequently back over my shoulder as we shuffle away, trying not to appear alarmed. But the bear doesn't follow, seeming content merely to have put us to flight. To have put us in our proper place. To have humbled arrogant man . . . "quietly refuting three thousand years of human dominion," as grizzly man

Doug "Hayduke" Peacock so well puts it in his wonderful
book *Grizzly Years*.

We hold no grudge against the bear for running us home
like a couple of school boys caught out late and spooked by
the approach of darkness. Encountering, *experiencing* an
adult grizzly at such close range, treading that magical seam
between daylight and dark in this primal, timeless country, is
a truly mystical experience. At least as close to one as I've ever
come. Or, I hope, am ever likely to come.

We plod homeward in the growing dark, finally reaching
camp, exhausted, just before midnight. We drop our packs
without bothering to unload them, wolf down a cold dinner
and retreat into our nylon and down cocoons.

Bruce is snoring almost instantly. But for me, sleep comes
reluctantly and even then is fraught with the timeless dreams
of wayfarers encamped far from home . . . vivid, compelling
visions of great antlered beasts, mystical bears, wood nymphs.

A new day: Through the gossamer walls of our nylon tent I
watch, bleary-eyed, as the sun struggles to climb free of a dark
shadow riding low on the eastern horizon—a bank of storm
clouds? I note a familiar but not particularly welcome sound,
like grains of sand being blown against the tent's rain fly. I
struggle from my sleeping bag, unzip the door flap and peer
out. The ground is salted with snow and more is falling. The
sharp cold air nips at my sleep-stiffened face.

Later, over mugs of strong camp coffee, Bruce and I discuss
yesterday's events, comparing what we have seen with our
own eyes concerning the habits of caribou, against what we
have read or heard from others. Having evolved under relent-
less pressure from such fearsome predators as grizzly bears
and wolves, you'd logically expect caribou to be watchful and
nervous creatures, though this is the antithesis of their reputation. Still, the seven animals with which we spent half of
yesterday did much to belie the almost bovine dullness often
attributed to their species.

As they fed along, one or more of their number was always on watch, head up, alert. When they bedded, they did so in the open, well away from any cover that predators, including the human variety, could use to conceal a close approach. And they further buffered their defense by bedding in a loose circle, each facing out so that every few degrees of direction were covered by at least one pair of eyes, one set of ears, one big attentive nose—the latter two senses on duty even as their proprietors napped. In all, Bruce and I agree as we look back on it now, the caribou we observed yesterday were neither as elusive as the wapiti that roam the mountains of my western home, nor as nervous as the ghostly whitetails of his eastern stamping grounds. Yet they were nobody's fools.

Dressed warmly, we eventually buck up our fortitude and walk the few dozen yards from our tent down to the river's edge to stand amidst the white falling flakes and cast pearlescent spinners at a hoped-for dinner of Arctic grayling.

They come at first in small bands—four, six, sometimes eight to the bunch—loafing down off the naked tundra, crashing through the tangle of autumn-yellowed alder and dwarf willow bordering the river, the tendons in their ankles clicking audibly, their hard keratin hooves clacking sharp and loud as they move boldly out onto the shore of glacial cobblestones. A moment's pause at water's edge to regroup and look around, then the leader (always for these crossings, we are learning, it's a gray old cow) leaps headlong into the deep frigid water, the rest of the band following close on her erect tail until the whole lot is lined out and swimming for the far shore.

Far shore for the caribou, near shore for Bruce and me. We wait here, crouching in the brush, our fishing rods laid hastily aside, watching the parade.

By noon the snow has stopped falling and perhaps a hundred animals—which we are hopeful will prove to be the vanguard of the local fall migration—have crossed the big Alaskan river in piecemeal fashion. Our hopes don't go

ungratified, for soon the open hillsides across the valley—
which just yesterday were void of visible animate life—are
swarming with the big brown-and-white deer. Dozens of
scattered bands appear on the horizon, link, and wander
down toward the river, funneling together as they come,
narrowing finally to a single long file as they approach the
ford.

In planning and imagining this trip, Bruce and I had hoped
to see something of this rare and wonderful sort, but hadn't
really expected to be so lucky; our timing is a bit early. But
now . . . hour after hour it continues, it builds, with breaks
between the crossing bands coming less often and growing
shorter in duration.

We take advantage of these hiatuses, as the need arises, to
hurry to the tent for cameras, film, snacks. I return to the river
after one such run to learn that I've just missed the brief
appearance of a young bull moose: The huge dark animal,
Bruce reports, ventured out onto the cobblestones, slurped up
a quick drink and melted back into the bush.

Likewise, once while Bruce is briefly away, a raft of a dozen
canvasbacks floats into view, riding the current hard against
the far shore, bobbing like so many feathery kayaks. Now and
again, a couple separates from the flock to chase one another
in a tight circle, necks outstretched, strong wings beating the
rippled surface of the river. When I rise slowly with aimed
camera, the ducks spot me immediately, take wing and fly low
and fast out of sight upstream.

It appears that Murphy's immutable law is at work even out
here in the Alaskan bush, for we are learning that the surest
way to stir up some wildlife action is for one of us to momentarily leave the river.

But the caribou, obliging souls they are, always announce
their arrival. Even inside our double-walled nylon shelter, with
the wind whining in the tall thin spruce that whisker up all
around the campsite, we know we're missing nothing—for
each time a new group of caribou approaches the ford, we
hear the noisome rattle of their hooves on the cobblestones,

the thunderous splashes of their big bodies plunging into the water, their constant low, gutteral, porcine grunts.

In the water, the swimming animals form a tight link of bobbing heads, backs and erect tails, a stepping-stone bridge across which my mind's eye pictures a swift and light-footed runner skipping lightly—from back to head to back—his quick sure feet stepping high and dry. I lapse momentarily into nostalgic recollections of myself as a younger man, a better animal. What is it they say . . . "Life is hard, then you die." Well, today I am very much alive. Never moreso.

Straight on the caribou come, bank to bank, neglecting to crab upstream as any knowledgeable river forder would do, yet losing not a yard to the swift current. Arrived, they clamber from the water and dry themselves by shaking vigorously, like so many big wet dogs.

On several occasions during the afternoon, various small groups of caribou attempt to land right in front of us, but turn quickly away when we rise from the brush to snap photographs. Confused but apparently not terribly frightened, the animals divert a short distance upstream to a less crowded landing, then climb out, shake and stand to stare and grunt their disgust at us before moving into the alders and out of sight.

Can this be the same wary species we played cat and mouse with out on the tundra just yesterday? It would seem that crowding and a herd instinct that commands all blindly to follow a designated leader combine to erode the native intelligence of individual caribou . . . much as similar circumstances often confound the common sense of individual human animals.

Later in the day, wanting a closer look, I dress in camouflage and ease into the shadowy world of riverside alder and willow. Guiding on a chorus of grunts and the pounding of hundreds of running hooves, I creep up a slough half a mile or so upriver from camp, at the head of which a seemingly endless line of caribou are landing.

In this dense brush I can see only a few yards in any direction, sometimes but a few feet, and am forced to bend and twist and squeeze my way between the slender, closely spaced trunks. Adding color and a certain nervous excitement to my stalk are occasional piles of grizzly droppings of indeterminable age (though, as I reckon it, not yet petrified and so hardly old enough)—big, soft, purple heaps shot through with the undigested seeds of berries and the remains of . . . God only knows.

But I meet no bears and, the wind in my favor, manage in the space of a few minutes to snake to within a breath-holding five yards of where a long line of just-landed animals is rounding a sharp right-hand bend on a narrow game trail, running flat-out. I assume a low profile, squatting on the ground just to the left of where the parade is turning right. Suddenly I come to the realization that should even one rugged individualist in the bunch decide to wheel left instead of right, running to the beat of his or her own drummer, as it were, and should those behind this rebel follow, I could emerge from this bold intrepid adventure looking not unlike one of those purple piles of putrid grizzly poop I dodged on the way in here.

But mine is not to worry, for, as I learned during our long riverside vigil near camp, migrating caribou are anything but independent. In fact, once a lead cow begins a crossing, her followers seem to lose all sense of individuality, all sense of direction, all sense of caution. All sense, period.

Why they run so frantically, so nose-to-tail mindlessly after emerging from a water crossing, I'm not qualified to say. But I can offer a guess or two: Maybe they feel insecure in these thick riverside alder jungles, their pace quickened by the threatening smell of bear dung. Perhaps none wants to be left behind, and so all rush forward in an attempt to overcome the accordion effect. Whatever the reason or reasons, while small groups of caribou roaming the open tundra, such as the seven Bruce and I dogged yesterday, can be almost as wary as woodlot whitetails, huge herds of the selfsame animals at river crossings appear to be little more clever or cautious than so many Herefords.

But they're certainly more graceful, infinitely more beautiful.

❦

Evening.

Night.

A new morning.

And still the caribou come.

Tens, hundreds have crossed since yesterday, continue to cross today—perhaps two thousand animals in all. A bounty of cervids it is, though but a small portion of the greater Mulchatna herd, estimated presently to number some sixty to seventy thousand antlered beasts.

And antlered beasts they are, all of them: bulls, cows—even the spring's crop of calves wear spike beams some half a foot long. All of the bulls, young and old alike, have finished antlers rubbed free of velvet and highly polished. The cows, however, their annual antler-growth cycle lagging somewhat behind that of the bulls, are still in velvet or just beginning to shed, a colorful few with long tatters of the skinlike tissue flapping like bloody pendants across their faces as they run, trailing down around their ears when they stop. The bared patches of new antler are still wet, shiny, crimson-stained.

Although an overwhelming majority of the animals we have seen thus far are cows, calves and young bulls, the really big boys have nonetheless been amply represented, some bearing antlers the likes of which I have never before seen, dwarfing even the fine rack we admired on that big bull out on the tundra a few of days ago.

And appropriately so. The huge Mulchatna herd, which makes its wide-ranging home inland and just north of the Alaska Peninsula, regularly produces some of the largest and most ornate racks to be found among the barren ground subspecies (*Rangifer tarandus granti*). Or, for that matter, among any of the five currently recognized North American caribou subspecies—the other four being the central-Canadian barren ground caribou (*R. t. groenlandicus*), the woodland caribou (*R. t. caribou*), the mountain caribou (*R. t. montanus*) and the Quebec-Labrador caribou (*Rangifer tarandus* of Quebec and Labrador).

Finally, sadly, as evening stretches its shadowy fingers across the tundra, the caribou thin out and cease coming. During the night we hear only an occasional splash in the river, a few grunts in the alders.

Come morning, only the eerie keening of the wind relieves the deep silence of this far-north country. Now, again, just as it was before the migration began, a full day's walk out across the tundra reveals no more than a few of the big cervids, scattered in singles, pairs, small bands. I have rarely felt so alone. Deserted. In spite of its beauty, such a place as this can be painfully lonely. In winter, it might as well be the moon.

❦

Here's a thought to ruminate: If you were a wild ungulate attempting to glean a wintertime living from the barren, snow-blanketed terrain of the arctic or subarctic north—what would you eat? Think about it: There'd be no grasses, sedges, buds, mushrooms, catkins, berries, leaves or herbs—all of which caribou eagerly devour spring through fall. Nothing much in sight but white punctuated with the spindly tops of willow and alder, and not near enough of that to go around.

What would you eat? Caribou survive winter after brutal winter by scenting (through snow depths of several inches), then using their hooves to dig down (as far as two feet) to uncover those low-growing communities of lichens and mosses that conspire to form the rich carpet of the vast arctic tundra.

Caribou feed widely on lichens, some sixty-two varieties, the year-round. But in winter, with most if not all other vegetation dead and gone, lichens are frequently just about *all* the northern caribou eat. Especially popular is one ubiquitous tundra species known appropriately as caribou (or reindeer) moss (*Cladonia rangiferina*).

Down in the lower forty-eight, the word "lichen" evokes visions of those low, scaly life forms that cling like stains to rocks and rotting logs. True enough, these are lichens. But there are more than sixteen thousand species of lichen worldwide, many of which are much more complicated and plantlike than the scaly varieties, though none of them produce flowers.

Take, for the most fitting example, the aforementioned caribou moss of the far north. This variety—all I have seen are white, gray, sage-green or beige in color—is an ornate, treelike little organism that commonly grows to a height of a couple of inches or so. One of the slowest growers in the plant kingdom, an inch-tall tundra lichen may be hundreds or even thousands of years old. (Some Greenland varieties are believed to survive in excess of four thousand years.)

At first glance, *Cladonia* resembles miniature sea coral. On closer inspection, however, giving only moderate rein to the imagination, the forking branches of this little plant hold a striking resemblance to the antlers of the animal for which it is named. Unique as snowflakes, no two branches of caribou lichen look exactly alike. But they do taste alike (yes, I tried it)—moist, bland, carrying perhaps just the slightest hint of mushroom. I wouldn't want to eat much of the stuff, and I pity those hard-pressed Arctic explorers I've heard of who, in survival situations, have been forced to.

Raw lichen (technically, a symbiotic community of two separate organisms, fungus and alga) is only marginally palatable to humans, difficult to digest and not very nutritious. But in the caribou's four-compartmented stomach, it is miraculously transformed into a nutritious, easily digested and pleasant tasting (so I've been told) source of wintertime greens much favored by Alaskan and Canadian natives, who know it as *nerrooks,* commonly referred to by caucasians as "Eskimo salad."

Unlike a horse, which has only one stomach and so must chew its food thoroughly before swallowing, and even at that is an inefficient digester, ruminants such as the cervids can bolt down huge quantities of barely chewed food, storing it in a paunch, or rumen. In this way, wild ruminants, all of which evolved as prey species, can limit the time they must spend exposed in open areas while feeding. Later, in the relaxed comfort and relative safety of a day bed, the stored meal is regurgitated, a snack at a time, in the form of a compressed wad, or cud. After a thorough chewing, the cud is reswallowed, this time bypassing the paunch and moving along to the stomach proper.

Thus, the magical ingredients that transform raw lichen into nutritious Eskimo salad include saliva and digestive juices from the caribou's complex stomach—decidedly unappetizing fare to effete Western palates. But hunger is the best sauce, and native hunters, after removing a quantity of *nerrooks* from the digestive plumbing of freshly killed caribou and allowing it to age for a few days, consume the greenish, healthful mush with gusto—a salad, indeed, to accompany their mainstay fare of rare red meat.

Winter is some easier for the woodland caribou, which inhabit the meteorologically more moderate, mature conifer forests extending from southern Canada down into the northwestern U.S. In the southern extreme of this range, a remnant couple of dozen animals make up the trans-border Selkirk herd of Canada and northern Idaho, forming the lower forty-eight's only known wild caribou herd. (Which, by the way, government wildlife managers have recently written off as no longer being worth the bother of trying to save. Too much interference with logging interests.)

For these southern caribou, eating in winter can be as effortless as nibbling at the long drapes of arboreal fruticose lichen—such as "old man's beard" (*Usnea*)—that hang like verdant cotton candy from the limbs of subalpine firs and old-growth Engelmann spruce. In this situation, deep snow—it accumulates to depths of twenty feet in some areas—is more of an aid than a plague to the caribou, since it provides a platform upon which they can walk to harvest the arboreal lichens that, in less snowy times, would wait—like the sour grapes of Aesopian fable—tauntingly just beyond their reach.

It is generally accepted that the genus of cervid we call caribou—the same genus, with slight physical and behavioral variations, is known in Eurasia as the reindeer—made its way across the Bering land bridge to North America sometime during the mid-Pleistocene, around a million years ago.

At face value, this would make the caribou possibly the most recent arrival of our four cervid genera. But the fossil record contains intriguing hints that *Rangifer* may have evolved originally in the Americas, with a portion of this seminal population eventually crossing to Eurasia. While the Eurasian immigrants prospered, so the theory goes, those that stayed behind gradually died out. Later, a portion of the Eurasian population recrossed and evolved slightly different characteristics from their Eurasian kin, thus accounting for the striking similarities among, as well as the distinct differences between, reindeer and caribou.

In size, caribou are larger than deer but smaller than elk and moose. A big barren ground bull might weigh six hundred pounds (273 kg), a cow 350 pounds (159 kg). But in absolute antler mass, the caribou is outshined only by the moose, and in antler-to-body-weight ratio by none. Further, the caribou is unique among cervids in that it is the only genus in which both sexes regularly carry antlers; of course, as you might expect, the headgear of the bulls is far larger, heavier and more ornate than that worn by caribou cows.

This difference in antler size correlates, by and large, with the disparity in body size between males and females, and therefore is to be expected. The real surprise is not that the cows' antlers are smaller, but that they have them at all. How can this be? And why? Most books discussing the cervids, both

popular and academic, fail to address this tricky question. Or
even to raise it. Still, there are hypotheses. Logical hypotheses.
Compelling hypotheses.

In our correspondence, Dr. Valerius Geist painted a caribou
scenario that corresponds with his general theories of cervid
evolution:

"Caribou females," Geist reasons, "grow antlers in line with
open-country adaptations, [and] open-country ungulates
generate male mimicry in females, so that females look like the
class of males they compete with for resources: Caribou females
resemble yearling up to 2-1/2-year-old bulls, whom they must
keep from their snow craters [pits used for feeding] in winter . . .
which are costly to excavate and are susceptible to being pirated
by the younger bulls. Note that female bison look like three-year-
old bulls; gnu females look like adult males, and etcetera [for
other open-country ungulate species]."

The Drs. Tony and George Bubenik, working independently
of (and occasionally at odds with) Valerius Geist, nonetheless
have arrived at strikingly similar opinions. From my correspondence with George Bubenik:

"We feel that much the best explanation for that capability
[antler-growing] is to make the females more competitive with
the males during the winter. Bull caribou cast their antlers
earlier than do the cows, leaving the antlered females better
able to compete for scarce food resources with the larger-
bodied but antlerless males.

"The physiological basis for antler development [in cow
caribou] is the relatively high level of androgens [male sex
hormones] in the blood of young females during the critical
[initial] period of pedicle development. The capability to grow
antlers exists in both sexes of cervids; if they possess sufficient
androgens at the proper time (at several months of age), they
will develop pedicles, from which antlers later will grow."

In a scientific paper published in a German-language
biological journal, the Bubeniks explored the subject of
neuro-endocrine regulation of the antler cycle. Here's an
edited translation of a pertinent section:

> In order for the pedicles to develop the
> first set of antlers, and to repeat antler
> growth annually, a special endocrine milieu
> [environment] is necessary. However, except
> in *Rangifer,* these special endocrine
> conditions appear only in males during a
> well-defined critical period [of early growth].

As scientifically enlightened and up-to-date as these hypotheses may be, diamond-in-the-rough observers had already scented and were following similar spoor more than a century ago, as the following excerpt from the 1882 publication *Three in Norway (by Two of Them),* by Jas. A. Lee and Walter J. Clutterbuck, attests:

> In the winter, when the "stor bocks" [large
> bulls] have no horns, the snow is often so
> deep that only the strongest Deer can scrape
> it away to lay bare the moss which at that
> season forms their food. Then come the does
> and smaller bucks, and with their horns push
> away the unfortunate big ones, and so are
> saved from starvation, while the ill-treated
> "stor bocks" have to work double tides in order
> to get anything to eat.

Adding further confusion to this most intriguing of antler mysteries is the fact that, while antlered females are virtually universal among the barren ground subspecies, they occur much less often among caribou races living farther south; one study determined that only five percent of the mature cows in a certain Newfoundland herd carried antlers. If we make the logical presumption that this phenomenon owes to the easier winters of the milder and more richly vegetated southerly habitat, allowing in turn a reduced competition for food among the members of a given herd, then the essentially parallel theories of Geist and the Bubeniks are in no way refuted, but in fact reinforced.

❧

As we have seen, the antlers of a mature bull caribou (aged five and beyond) are palmate, with the main beams curving out and forward to a maximum length of sixty inches (1.52 m) or so. But the most interesting and unusual characteristic of caribou antler form is the "shovel"—a broadly palmated brow tine that aligns vertically and centers over the animal's muzzle, often reaching down to or even beyond the tip of the nose. In rare instances, both brow tines will follow this pattern, creating the "double shovel" so coveted by trophy hunters.

Folk tradition has it that caribou bulls use these shovels to excavate snow craters for winter feeding. But such behavior has never been scientifically, nor even credibly, documented. Moreover, since male caribou begin casting their antlers as early as the latter part of November, and the overwhelming majority have gone bald by late December, the animals are without their shovels during the most severe snow months each winter—a pragmatic refutation of the snow-shoveling myth.

But if not for moving snow, than what purpose *do* these palmate oddities serve?

It seems likely that the shovel has the same functional purpose as the brow tines of other cervids—eye protection during sparring contests. Additionally and probably, the shovel could also serve some esoteric purpose of visual communication—as, in general, do all parts of all antlers when perceived as a whole, or *gestalt,* by a conspecific.

But to the human species, animal in fact yet largely deaf to the symbolic language of our nonhuman fellow creatures, the caribou's shovel is just another of evolution's mysterious and graceful embellishments to organs already so bizarre, so ornate, so unlikely as to defy our imaginations and confound our comprehension.

**CARIBOU DISTRIBUTION**

# ❧ V.

## OF *MEGALOCEROS* AND MIRACLES
### *The Biggest Antlers of All*

> Antlers are an extravagance of nature, rivalled only
> by such other biological luxuries as flowers, butterfly
> wings, and peacock tails.
>
> —RICHARD J. GOSS
> from *Deer Antlers*

WE COME NOW TO the question of diversity: Why do some deer
species have small (relative to body size), rather plain antlers,
while others, such as moose and caribou, have such huge,
stately, ornate racks?

Of the various hypotheses that have been developed in an
attempt to answer this and other particularly slippery questions of cervid evolutionary variety, one stands—at least in this
student's judgment—heads above all the rest. This is the "dispersal" hypothesis developed by the University of Calgary's
Dr. Valerius Geist, a world-renowned expert on antlered and
horned mammals and author of the definitive academic work
on wild sheep, *Mountain Sheep: A Study in Behavior and
Evolution*.

The Geist dispersal hypothesis maintains that during those
cycles in Ice Age times (a period that came to a close around
eleven thousand years ago) when the living was relatively
easy and, consequently, wildlife populations were high, some
of the more adventurous groups of mammals inhabiting the
outskirts of their species' home ranges tended to wander,
extending their kind into new and often far-flung territories.
Many of these fresh stamping grounds were located at

temperate latitudes and elevations, where the "productivity pulse" was long—that is, where the season of rapid vegetation growth was generous. It was under these happy circumstances, Valerius Geist maintains, that a great deal of speciation—the splitting off and evolvement of new forms from old—took place.

With an abundance of food and a lack of crowding in their ever-new surroundings, members of these wandering and colonizing populations not only grew larger of body, but were required to spend less time foraging or grazing and so had more time and energy available to devote to developing complex social patterns (not a conscious effort mind you, but merely a natural tendency)—in particular, those social patterns involving competition for breeding privileges.

The development of any physical or behaviorial (social) modification that helped an animal improve its chances of mating successfully thus would have been encouraged—both in the individual in which it initially occurred as well as in offspring. And since more complex social patterns demand more complex forms of communication, various "luxury" (non-life-essential) organs that served as visual rutting cues would have enjoyed an accelerated evolution.

In the deer family, these organs of social communication developed according to a pattern biologists call polarity, wherein intraspecific (same-species) visual cues drifted to the body's extremes, or "poles": to the head as antlers, and to the hindmost as light-colored rump patches and tails (or, more often, undertails).

While starvation would have been no great threat in such fat and rapidly evolving circumstances, predators most likely would have been a constant nemesis. Thus, those individuals most physically and genetically capable of avoiding and escaping predation would have courted evolutionary favor. Specifically, they would have tended to live longer than their less fit mates, thereby gaining additional time for both reproduction and the growth of larger and more ornate luxury organs. As a consequence, larger antlers—which correlate with large, strong, mature (more survival-prone) bodies—assumed ever-greater importance both as symbols of social status and as indicators of physical and genetic fitness.

Imagine this process at work over a very long period of time and under varying circumstances in widespread locations, and the origins of many of the large number of highly evolved and significantly distinct deer species and subspecies we know today, as well as the differences in the antlers they wear—become clear.

After reading a seminal draft of this chapter, Dr. Geist commented in a written critique, "You may note that the productivity pulse length reverses at about sixty degrees north, so that body size in ungulates declines beyond that latitude; caribou [North America's northern-most deer type] are smaller below and above that general latitude."

Those familiar with biology will recognize how this dovetail's with a phenomenon known as Bergmann's rule, which states that, by and large, the farther north or south of the equator a species lives, the larger of body it tends to be. The evolutionary purpose (or, more accurately, result) here is one of heat retention: The larger an animal's body, the smaller its relative surface area; and the smaller the relative surface area, the less body heat is radiated (and so lost) to a chill atmosphere.

Interpreting Bergmann's rule in reverse, we would expect those creatures living in warmer climates, nearer the equator, to be generally smaller of body, thereby increasing their relative surface areas in order to give off more body heat in an effort to stay cooler. And so it is.

Thus, the evolution of Ice Age mammals living during fat cycles tended toward giantism—in conformation with, though not necessarily in servitude to, Bergmann's rule. Meanwhile, the evolution of species living during lean Ice Age cycles, Geist's dispersal hypothesis proposes, tended toward physical conservatism, particularly in latitudes and elevations having short productivity pulses.

The extreme examples of this trend to moderation are those species that became isolated on small islands with limited resources and no pressure from predators. (Where they existed, predators would quickly have eradicated the entire marooned prey population and, in the doing, starved themselves into extinction.) In such dire straits, the object of the game wouldn't be to outshine your physical, social and breeding competition by becoming fleeter, smarter or larger and more beautiful of body. Rather, it would be to assure getting enough food in your belly to allow you to mature and have the strength and opportunity to breed at all.

How best to accomplish that end? By minimizing your physical needs. That is, by reducing the size of any energy-robbing nonessential or luxury organs; by reducing the size, even, of your very body.

It is with this in mind that Valerius Geist hypothesizes (and not without evidence to back him up) that Ice Age cervid populations living under sparse and isolated conditions tended to pursue survival strategies that promoted what could be called, for the sake of convenience, *reverse* evolution—a return to smaller, simpler forms. The antlers of such species tended to shrink. Body size diminished as well, and social interaction declined. The Florida Key deer, the most diminutive member of the whitetail clan and, in fact, the smallest deer native to North America, is a living example of both this "reverse" evolutionary process and the workings of Bergmann's rule.

In addition to accounting for the diversity of cervid species, the dispersal hypothesis would also appear to help plug a slow and bothersome leak in the hull of traditional evolutionary theory—a leak that anti-evolutionists (better known as creationists) have long pointed to with self-righteous glee.

That leak is this: If evolution is a slow, steady progression from primitive forms to modern—a progression sometimes likened to ascending the rungs of a stepladder (an analogy Darwin never used, though many of his philosophical descendants since have)—why then doesn't the fossil record reflect

same? Why are there so many missing rungs in the evolutionary ladder? Why, that is, do there exist so many gaps in the
geological record of evolution, indicating an apparent lack of
smooth transitions between old forms and new? Where are the
missing links?

Until recently, the evolutionist's best answer to this pesky
but pregnant question has been that the geological record is
far from fully exposed to examination. Only a few pages of the
big book of time have been opened—via faults, upthrusts,
erosion and other geological workings—while the rest remain
sealed beneath the earth's crust.

While it is true that geological action has made available for
scientific inspection only a fragment of the full evolutionary
story, enough nonetheless is known to determine that apparent gaps do in fact exist; the fossil record of evolution is far
from smooth and continual. Surely even the staunchest of
evolutionists, deep in his pragmatic heart, must have long
suspected that such an explanation was inadequate and
longed for more.

Now, with the advent of the dispersal hypothesis and re-
lated theories, a large portion of this unsettling mystery may at
last be solved. In Geist's words, from a paper titled "On
Speciation in Ice Age Mammals, with Special Reference to
Cervids and Caprids," published in *The Canadian Journal of
Zoology,* (Vol. 65, 1987):

> Major climatic changes giving rise to colonization
> should give rise simultaneously to many new species.
> Since speciation is tied to dispersal, one cannot
> expect to find the [fossil remains of an] ancestral
> species with [the fossil remains of] a descendent
> species in the same geographical area. Consequently,
> new species appear seemingly out of "nowhere."

In other words, during Ice Age times, mobile, colonizing
groups of established cervid forms moved on to newer and
greener pastures where, under favorable circumstances, they
evolved—which is to say, they *changed*—with striking
rapidity relative to the normal progress of such doings. For this

reason, new forms pop up at times and in locations far removed from fossils representing eons of evolutionary stability among the parent forms. When revealed in the fossil record, this leaves the false impression that the new forms simply materialized or, if you prefer, were created, without benefit of transitional forms—those troublesome missing links.

Valerius Geist's dispersal hypothesis may help explain the origins of the many and great differences between antler types in various deer species, but it doesn't entirely explain the evolution of really *big* antlers. While the theory outlines the circumstances that would have been conducive to rapid speciation, enhanced antler development and increased size and ornateness of luxury organs in general, it doesn't specifically address the questions of why and how giant antlers came about. But no matter, for the industrious Dr. Geist has another, related hypothesis that strives to do just that.

To best understand Geist's "big-antler" hypothesis, it helps first to get to know the largest-antlered deer ever to have lived. This was *Megaloceros giganteus,* the extinct so-called "Irish elk."

We know from skeletal remains that a mature *Megaloceros* stag stood to more than seven feet at the shoulders and would have weighed perhaps in excess of 1,500 pounds (682 kilos). The antlers carried by the grandest of these great beasts weighed some ninety-five to 110 pounds (forty-three to fifty kilos), occasionally more, often exceeding six feet (1.83 meters) in length and spanning as much as 168 inches (4.27m) tip to tip. That's a spread, you realize, of fourteen *feet.*

Think of it. The greatest beam-to-beam spread on record for modern elk is a comparatively humble 63.5 inches (1.61m). Moreover, the mass of the Irish elk's antlers was increased greatly by being palmate—wide and flattened, resembling huge hands with the fingers spread—as are those of modern moose, caribou, fallow deer and others.

This outrageous headgear ranks as the most massive ever worn by any animal, extinct or living, and is almost double that of the largest moose alive today. Early on, in fact, it was presumed from the general shape, palmate structure and great size of its antlers and body that the Irish elk *was* a moose. The poor dead creature is popularly referred to as an elk rather than a moose because "elk" (from the ancient Greek *alce,* which found its way into the German as *elch* and finally into English as "elk") is what Europeans call the animal we here in North America know as the moose (they call their elk, you'll remember, "red deer").

But no matter, for the extinct ruminant was no more a moose than it was an elk. What it was, Geist's studies have convinced him and others, was an early relative of today's Eurasian fallow deer (genus *Dama*).

Further, the Irish elk was Irish only insofar as Irish peat bogs were the first locales to yield its antlers (in 1588) and remain today the richest repositories. Even so, many antlers and some entire *Megaloceros* skeletons have been exhumed in England, Germany and many far-flung elsewheres. Because the Irish elk was designed for life in a temperate climate, it never wandered to the extremes of Siberia and on across the Bering land bridge to North America, as did deer, moose, caribou and wapiti.

The Irish elk was perhaps half a million years in evolving to the highly specialized form that flourished during the late Pleistocene, a rich Ice Age time of generalized giantism in mammals. In its final millennium, eleven to twelve thousand years ago, it roamed in great herds across vast, well-watered grasslands, living and lusting and reproducing its eccentric genes for a relatively short while before joining the silent ranks of the vanished.

Neither bluff, battle nor beauty, however, would seem to fully explain the need for headgear the awesome likes of that worn by *Megaloceros*. What, then, might have been natural selection's purpose (which is to say, *justification*) for such giant antlers?

The answer, as I reckon it, begins with an extinct Englishman named Thomas Malthus.

Thomas Malthus was a British social economist of the late eighteenth and early nineteenth centuries. In 1798 he published a book titled (in severely abbreviated form) *An Essay on the Principle of Population.* Therein, this clear-sighted and compassionate man offered a revolutionary theory on the nature of population growth as it relates to the fate of humanity.

In brief, what Malthus said was that human populations can reproduce themselves geometrically (one plus one equals two, two plus two equals four, four plus four equals eight and etcetera). Meanwhile, the means of production of food and other necessities can be increased only arithmetically (one plus one equals two, two plus one equals three, three plus one equals four and so on). Therefore, cautioned Malthus, unless humans take voluntary steps to hold their population to within what the earth can comfortably support *over the long haul,* pressure on the environment will increase until nature is forced to step in and limit our population *for* us, via such "natural" disasters as famine, drought and disease, as well as their spin-off—war.

Malthus was right, of course; the proof screams its horrible affirmation throughout the so-called Third World today. But what has all or any of this to do with big antlers?

That's where a second extinct Englishman, Charles Darwin, enters the picture. In his autobiography, Darwin recalls how, in 1838, a casual reading of Malthus's *Essay on the Principle of Population* precipitated a breakthrough in his thinking about the origin and evolution of species:

> I happened to read for amusement Malthus on
> *Population,* and being well prepared to
> appreciate the struggle for existence which
> everywhere goes on from long continued
> observation of the habits of animals and plants,
> it at once struck me that under these circumstances
> favorable variations would tend to be preserved and
> unfavorable ones to be destroyed. The result of
> this would be the formation of new species.

There we have an embryonic sketch of the workings of evolution via natural selection. In his remarkable treatise *The Origin of Species,* published in 1859, Darwin expanded on those early musings:

> Amongst many animals, sexual selection will
> have given its aid to ordinary selection, by
> assuring to the most vigorous and best adapted
> males the greatest number of offspring. . . . But
> success will often depend on the males having
> special weapons, or means of defense, or charms;
> and a slight advantage will lead to victory.

In the deer family, of course, those special male weapons and charms are antlers. In the exceptional cases of the Irish elk, the North American moose and a few other species, however, we are still left to wonder at the necessity for *such* weapons and charms. Might not the disadvantages inherent to their great bony bulk—weight, clumsiness, nutritional drain—more than counterbalance any advantages they might bring to the survival of the individual and, it follows, the survival and refinement of the species, by enhancing the processes of selective reproduction?

A good, convoluted question, this though maybe not quite so good (though every bit as convoluted) as it was back in Darwin's day.

In an article appearing in the March, 1986 issue of *Natural History,* Valerius Geist struck again, outlining his groundbreaking theory—the theory I've been pecking around the edges of here—concerning the evolvement of outsized antlers:

> The solution to the mystery of [the Irish
> elk's] huge antlers lies, paradoxically, in the
> giant deer's adaptation to running. Running with
> great speed and endurance is a means of evading
> predators and requires a large amount of space.
> For this trait to promote survival, the young
> must be as fleet-footed as their mothers soon
> after birth. Offspring must be born as large and

as highly developed as possible and fed a supply
of milk abundant enough in nutrients and energy
to foster rapid growth to "survival size," thus
shortening the vulnerable time period after birth. . . .
  To produce milk rich in nutrients and energy,
the mother needs to select highly nutritious and
digestible forage, and above all, she must be able
to divert these nutrients and energy from body
growth and maintenance to milk production. In
males, the same genetic ability to divert nutrients
means that more material is available for antler
growth. . . . A female choosing a male with relatively
large antlers selects one with a hereditary endow-
ment for superior foraging and for diverting nutrients
and energy from body growth to antler production. *

In summary, then, Geist is saying that the relative size of
cervid young at birth, the percentage of milk solids produced
by lactating females and antler size in males all show positive
correlation with a species' proclivity for and competence in
long-distance running. Thus, according to this innovative
hypothesis, giant antlers evolved as an intraspecific indication—that is, an advertisement to eligible females within the
same species—of a male cursorial (running) deer's ability to
utilize its environment efficiently.

We see many of these same traits today in the caribou, an
open-country species whose first defense against predators
(primarily wolves) is running. Caribou display all three of
Geist's definitive characteristics of giant-antlered cervids, both
living and extinct: very large, ornate antlers in mature males;
the production of exceptionally rich milk in mature females
(the caribou cow produces the richest milk, in point of fact, of
any living cervid species); and large birth size and rapid
growth in the young (a healthy ten- to twenty-pound caribou
calf, born in late May or early June, will be able to follow its
mother within an hour of birth, and capable of keeping up
with its herd's rapid roamings within a couple of days).

--------

* (With permission from *Natural History,* Volume 95, Number 3; Copyright The
American Museum of Natural History, 1986.)

Meanwhile, smaller-antlered deer and elk evolved different survival strategies suited to their differing environments. Rather than making their homes on vast grasslands, as did the Irish elk, or out on the treeless tundra, as do the caribou, deer and elk are primarily dwellers of adolescent (as opposed to old-growth) forests and brushy edges. And since forest-dwelling cervids don't roam in large herds (notwithstanding that deer and elk sometimes congregate, of necessity, on winter feeding grounds), the newborns of deer and elk have evolved to evade the hungry jaws of predators—not by fleeing, as do the young of caribou and other cursorial species, but by lying low, hiding, while the mother watches from nearby, ready to provide whatever defense or diversion she can.

(Just this past summer, while hiking with a friend up an oak-brush hillside near my cabin, a large doe stood from just ahead of us, trotted a short distance, then stopped broadside at a distance of no more than twenty yards. When we failed to give chase—as instinct would suggest to her we should—she actually minced a few paces *toward* us. From previous experience—identical experience under identical circumstances on this selfsame hillside a few years ago—I knew she had a fawn or fawns stashed somewhere nearby. My friend and I detoured around the bold doe, who, after watching us for a while longer, slunk back down into the nursery brush. The next time I traversed that hillside, a couple of days later, the doe was gone; as I had expected, she had wisely moved her kinder to a quieter neighborhood.)

Because of this hiding instinct, deer and elk can afford to be born smaller relative to the size of adults of their species, which in fact they are, and to mature more slowly than caribou calves, which they do. Because of this—and here it all comes together—their mothers can afford to be less efficient browsers, and to produce milk of moderate richness compared to the cursorial species. In the males, these same semi-sedentary traits are reflected, in compliance with Geist's big-antler hypothesis, in smaller antlers. (While the elk's antlers are high, wide and handsome, they nonetheless lack the great palmate mass and relative size of Irish elk or caribou racks.)

The moose is something of an in-between species. Although the big cervid originally evolved for a cursorial lifestyle, it has, in modern times, become primarily a dweller of Boreal forests. This, taken together with the fact that moose young hide as newborns, leads a tracker of the Geist theory to expect the richness of moose milk to be lower than that of caribou—which it handily is, falling in with that of deer and elk, the other "hiders." Moreover, the moose's antlers, while larger than those of deer and elk, should be smaller than those grown by caribou—which they don't appear to be, and which apparent anomaly we shall address forthwith.

By the evidence so far presented, we are led to expect greater evolutionary pressure for the development of big antlers in the Irish elk and the caribou, those two quintessential open-country runners, than in the forest-dwelling species such as deer, elk and moose. Why, then, aren't the caribou's antlers larger than those of the moose?

The answer is deceptively simple: In relation to body size, caribou antlers *are* larger—two to three times larger than those of the moose.

In accordance with a biological phenomenon known as allometry, antler size increases not just in proportion to body size, but faster (Dr. Geist reckons $1 \cdot 35$ in the exponent). Thus, the racks of large deer species aren't just *absolutely* larger than those of smaller cervids, but *relatively* larger as well. A big bull caribou might weigh six or seven hundred pounds on the hoof, while a whopper Alaska-Yukon bull moose will easily double, almost triple that weight. Thus, the forest-dwelling moose's antlers are more massive than those of the tundra-running caribou only because the animal itself is so very much larger.

Until recently, many biologists considered the Irish elk's outsized antlers to have been the primary cause of the species' eventual demise—a fatal evolutionary mistake, as it were. Surely, it was thought, such monstrous organs would rob the animal's body of important nutrients, make fording rivers and lakes more difficult and dangerous and tend to get hung up in brush and trees, hindering escape from predators.

As logical as this all may sound, it apparently was not the case. The antlers of the Irish elk, like those of moose and the other big-racked deer species, were no mistake, but evolved in positive response to specific needs.

The real undoing of the Irish elk was not its gigantic antlers, but its entrenched specialization and consequent lack of adaptability. The rapidly changing climate at the close of the final great glaciation stole away the open grasslands on which the giant grazers depended for their survival. Unable to adapt quickly enough to the life and diet of either tundra or forest, hounded certainly by natural predators and, in some areas, most probably by early human hunters as well, one of nature's most bizarre and grand creations ever, like MacArthur's proverbial old soldier, just . . . faded . . . away.

# BIG-ELK STORIES

> Has joy any survival value in the operation of
> evolution? I suspect that it does; I suspect that the
> morose and fearful are doomed to quick extinction.
> Where there is no joy there can be no courage; and
> without courage all other virtues are useless.
>
> —Edward Abbey
> from *Desert Solitaire*

EVEN THOUGH THE antlers grown by today's wapiti—the "true" elk—are no match for the monolithic headgear produced by the extinct Irish elk, they are nonetheless in many ways special, and particularly so a couple of pair I've come to know and love. Here are their stories.

### BIG-ELK STORY ONE

On a chill fall morning during the waning days of the nineteenth century—the year 1899 is often mentioned—a lone hunter ventured into an angular patch of Colorado geography having the foreboding name of Dark Canyon; to be precise, the Dark Canyon of Anthracite Creek, just north of Kebler Pass, deep in what is now west-central Colorado's Gunnison National Forest. The hunter, name of John Plute, had come for elk, riding out the dozen or so miles from his home in a high-country mining town with the picture-perfect name of Crested Butte (now a bustling ski and mountain biking town).

A hard-rock miner by profession, John Plute's recreational passion was hunting, an activity at which he was obviously proficient. Even so, he was not a "trophy hunter," per se. Excepting Teddy Roosevelt (with whom Plute once in fact hunted) and a relative handful of generally urban others, few people were interested in antlers back then. Rather, like most men of his time and station, John Plute hunted for meat—meat to fill his own belly and to barter around for goods and services.

Still, the antlers of the bull elk John Plute killed with his .30-40 Krag in Dark Canyon that fall day nearly a century ago were so extraordinarily huge and comely that he went to the considerable labor of packing the weighty appendages, together with several hundred pounds of elk meat, back to town. There, the amazing antlers were for a time admired then, so the story goes, stored away in a shed and all but forgotten. Around 1915, Plute gave the antlers to his friend John Rozich, owner of Crested Butte's appropriately named Elk Saloon. (Not, as some speculative journalists have written, to satisfy a bar bill, but simply because the two men were close friends. Being a bachelor who lived alone in a boarding house, Plute had no place of his own to display the ample rack.) Rozich promptly mounted the antlers over his bar, which would wear them for the next four decades.

In 1922, at age 54, John Plute died after being thrown from a horse. When John Rozich followed Plute to the grave in 1947, the Elk Saloon and its antlers went to his stepsons, Ed and Tony Rozman.

In 1955, the Rozman brothers measured the antlers using an official Boone and Crockett Club score sheet. However, this being their first effort at trophy scoring—a tricky business even for veteran measurers—they neglected to subtract penalty points for differences in symmetry between right and left sides, and so over-scored the head at an incredible 460 points. When B&C headquarters, then located in New York, saw that astronomic figure, they requested that the rack be measured by one of their designated scorers. It took three years for that to happen, and of course the 460 didn't hold up. But the B&C

brass were nonetheless sufficiently impressed to ask that the antlers be sent to New York for official panel measurement. With the financial assistance of the nearby Hotchkiss Elks Lodge, the Plute rack departed Colorado forthwith.

In 1962—seven years after the process had been timidly initiated and more than six decades since the trophy was taken—John Plute's Dark Canyon bull was declared the world record North American elk.

According to the Boone and Crockett Club's *Records of North American Big Game,* the Dark Canyon head scores a total 442-3/8 points—"points" being equivalent to inches derived from an exacting series of measurements. The right main beam is 55-5/8 inches in length and sprouts eight long tines—one to a length of 27-3/8 inches. Circumference of the right beam at the slimmest point between brow (first, or lowest) and bez (second) tines is 12-1/8 inches. The left beam is exactly four inches longer than the right, but carries one less tine and measures a slightly less beefy 11-2/8 inches around. The widest inside spread is 45-4/8 inches. (In case you're wondering, in the Boone and Crockett scoring system, fractions are recorded to the nearest 1/8-inch without reduction. Thus, the 45-1/2-inch spread of the Dark Canyon elk is recorded as 45-4/8 points.)

What of the Dark Canyon rack today?

A few years ago, Ed Rozman—now retired to nearby Paonia, Colorado—was quoted as saying that people had offered him as much as fifty thousand dollars for the mount, but that it's not for sale. Rozman does, however, occasionally loan the antlers out for public display under the care of an exceedingly conscientious guardian—the Rocky Mountain Elk Foundation, a large and active hunter-conservationist organization headquartered at Missoula, Montana.

When at home, the world's top typical (that is, having few or no nontypical or "freak" features) North American elk hangs much of each winter (ski season) in the Crested Butte Motor Inn, operated by Ed Rozman's nephews, Richard and Rudy.

When not there, the head can often be found at a vintage hardware store and gas station owned by Rozman's good old friend (and stepfather-in-law), Tony Milhelich, where it hangs alongside a photograph of John Plute.

It was at Tony's, matter of fact, where I, like thousands of others before and since, first gawked at the Plute head. That would have been, let's see, nearly a quarter of a century ago. Since then, I've been fortunate enough to see, admire and ponder this natural masterpiece on several more occasions. Each time, my reactions are the same: amazement, wonder. Why, in more than ninety years, hasn't another rack of this size and quality turned up in the record books? And carrying that query a step further, what are the growth factors that would have to come together to produce a set of antlers that would meet or beat the Dark Canyon record?

The answer to the first question is self-evident: Given time and favorable circumstances, anything that has occurred previously in the recent history of evolution conceivably can occur again. (In fact, a set of cast antlers was found recently on the San Carlos Apache Reservation in Arizona that measures slightly *larger* than the Dark Canyon rack, though the animal that produced them has yet to be identified, and the record books do not accept cast antlers since the spread between beams—a critical measurement—cannot be accurately determined unless the antlers remain attached to the skull that produced them. Unlikely as it seems—given that it's in largest part a desert state—it is widely believed that the next world record elk will come from Arizona.)

Concerning the factors necessary to produce a new world record—one man who knows is the Rocky Mountain Elk Foundation's Dr. Gary Wolfe, former wildlife manager and biologist for the nearly half-million-acre Vermejo Park Ranch in New Mexico and Colorado. During his twelve years there, in addition to other research projects, Wolfe conducted a pioneering study of the factors controlling the production of trophy-quality antlers in wild Rocky Mountain elk. These factors are: genetics, nutrition, health and age.

Assuming the first three to be adequate—which, at Vermejo Park, they generally are—Wolfe feels that the fourth ingredient, age, is the critical variant. In his own words, excerpted from the article "Old Elk, Trophy Elk," published in the Fall 1984 issue of *Bugle* (the quarterly RMEF journal), Wolfe explains:

> In [my] study, antler length, circumference and weight peaked in bulls 10-1/2 years old. However, the average number of antler points reached a maximum at 7-1/2 years of age, and remained relatively stable for several years. This suggests that although maximum antler point development occurs by 7-1/2 years of age, bulls continue to grow larger antlers for several successive years by adding length and mass, rather than additional points.
>
> I believe that the small number of elk in the record books [relative to other cervid species] is primarily due to the fact that most bulls are killed before they reach physical maturity, and never have a chance to express their genetic potential.
>
> Assuming there are no nutritional, genetic or health problems, the task of increasing the number of trophy elk in a given area is essentially one of reducing the harvest of bull elk and shifting more bulls into the older age classes.
>
> The most desirable solution is to simply reduce the number of hunters in selected management units. This should reduce the harvest and allow more bulls to live long enough to reach the 7-1/2 to 10-1/2 age classes.
>
> This departs from the traditional game management approach of maintaining young age-class herds which provide maximum harvestable surpluses.

In personal correspondence, Wolfe added a proviso, saying: "My intention is not to downplay the importance of genetics or nutrition, but simply to point out that in most North American elk herds, trophy animals are rare due to the skewed age ratios resulting from heavy hunting pressure.

"Of the four factors (age, genetics, nutrition and health status), wildlife managers are most able to affect age structure—via hunting regulations. This is not to imply that *all* old elk produced by restrictive hunting regulations will be trophies. Many elk will never produce trophy antlers, regardless of how long they live or the quality of their nutrition—they simply don't have the genetic potential. However, if a bull is killed at a young age, then it never has the opportunity to reach the maximum antler development possible within its genetic potential."

With this knowledge, it becomes obvious that the primary reason North America has failed to produce more elk racks on a par with the turn-of-the-century Dark Canyon bull is hunting pressure. Modern hunters—armed with ever-improving firearms and coached with the expert advice of volumes of written, recorded and even videotaped hunting lore—have become so much more effective in their pursuits that public-lands bulls surviving to peak antler-producing age have become as scarce as fur on a fish.

In light of this, it seems self-evident that adding more mature, big-antlered bulls to our public-lands herds would be a godsend—not just for hunters—but for the hunted as well, since the vast majority of elk herds today are critically under-staffed with prime breeding bulls. By managing elk and regulating hunting to produce a greater number and percentage of mature bulls, wildlife professionals would be working toward the parallel goals of improving hunting while also strengthening the genetic health and general welfare of the species.

Still, few things worthwhile are easily accomplished, and consistent, unvarying management policies having as their single-minded goal the enhancement of the quality and quantity of trophy bulls, while perhaps beneficial in the short run, won't necessarily prove out over the long haul to establish and maintain the *social balance* necessary for the ongoing welfare of the species.

In a courageous essay titled "An Immodest Proposal," published in the Fall 1988 issue of *Bugle,* Dr. Tony Bubenik tackled this tricky problem. First explaining the biological importance of establishing and maintaining social balance within wild cervid populations, he then laid out those factors that work for and against establishing and maintaining such a balance. Finally, Bubenik outlined his innovative and controversial concept for the long-term management of North America's antlered species.

Here, condensed from that article, is the gist of Bubenik's immodest but far-sighted and promising proposal:

> As our most important game management tool, hunting regulations should spell out not just the number of animals killed per year in a given area, but the social classes of those animals as well. In formulating these regulations, wildlife managers should ask the following questions: Is a given elk population living well, or is it suffering social misery? If the latter, what needs to be done to restore social order? That is, how many and which classes of an unbalanced population are potential trouble makers in a sociobiological sense (in technical jargon, supernumeraries)? Once these classes are identified, they should be targeted for culling by hunters.
>
> If, in some cases, these targeted supernumeraries turn out to be trophy-class bulls in or beyond prime breeding age, we, as hunters, are in luck. If not, then we as men and women who care about the long-term welfare of our elk resource must learn to place our personal desires behind the needs of the resource.
>
> In order to survive as long as it has, North America's deer family long ago had to develop social rules or mechanisms that would keep both the herds and their individual members fit and competitive. This they accomplished with grand success. However, when regulations allow hunters to cull certain classes of a population's members (with elk, it's most often spikes and trophy bulls)

in an unscientific, catch-as-catch-can manner,
the herd's social mechanisms can become
dangerously stressed. This is exactly the fix
we're in today. Why the urge to fill our tags
with the first legal animal we can find, or, conversely, with only trophy bulls? Why not go
afield to enjoy, to observe, to track, to experiment
with bugling, to fool and educate inexperienced
bulls while searching for—not necessarily a trophy—
but a member of the class that needs to be culled
from the herd being hunted?

In summary, social imbalances in an elk
population threaten both the quantity and
quality of its members. To [restore social balance]
will require management practices more scientific,
flexible and progressive than those traditionally
and currently in use—practices that may never be
accepted and implemented without the encouragement and support of a great many selfless, far-sighted
hunters.

Once established, such socially-balanced herds
would enjoy high enough rates of reproduction and
calf survival that long and generous hunting seasons
would be required to handle the annually occurring
abundance of various classes of supernumeraries—
in order to keep the herd size and social makeup in
balance.

This idyllic concept, as promising as it sounds, probably will
never be implemented. State game departments have enough
trouble just getting the general hunting public to understand and cooperate with the present and sufficiently
confusing antler regulations—to be fair to the hunters, it's
damn hard to tell a three-by-three mule deer from a four-by-
four, or a five-by elk from a six-by, under field conditions. To
try and get hunters to select a specific age and class of game
animal in the split-second that's often available . . . well, not
many are up to it.

### ✒ BIG-ELK STORY TWO

It's not hard to find the Horn Hut in tiny Creede, Colorado (population: 610). As you enter town on state highway 149, watch for the Mucker's Bucket Saloon on your right. Take the first left past the Bucket, then left again on Creede Avenue, and you'll see it there out the driver's-side window—a small, brown, barn-style structure all but hidden behind a walk-through arch of weather-bleached antlers.

Step into the Horn Hut, as I did for the first time just over a year ago, and you're stepping into a wonderland of antler art—cases and shelves brimming with bolas, buckles, buttons, chandeliers, earrings, knives, pendants, candle holders, cribbage boards, even furniture—each piece crafted by the talented hands of the Horn Hut's proprietor, George Carpenter.

But not all of the Horn Hut's antlers have been cut and polished. High on the walls all around hangs a crowd-stopping collection of indigenous Rocky Mountain fish and game mounts, including some beautifully antlered elk and deer. It's a veritable natural history museum. Each of the several antler mounts is special, but the prize of the lot is a massive, dark-stained elk rack with nine points on the right beam, seven on the left, and a freak double right brow tine. This head will, as they say, flat knock your socks off.

From the moment I first set eyes on what I have come to call the Horn Hut rack, I was hooked. I yearned to know more— the Boone and Crockett measurements for starters. When and where the bull was killed. The name of the hunter and his story.

The first of those questions was answered promptly, if not conclusively, by scanning a B&C score sheet handed me by George; it had been filled out, he said, by a knowledgeable, albeit not B&C sanctioned, Colorado Division of Wildlife officer. It appeared from this score sheet that while the mighty John Plute antlers beat out the Horn Hut rack in length of tines (significantly) and main beams (barely), the latter dominated in number of tines and circumference of main beams. Like so:

|                                                              | **Plute Head**          | **Horn Hut Rack**        |
| ------------------------------------------------------------ | ----------------------- | ------------------------ |
| Number of points on each antler                              | R = 8, L = 7            | R = 9, L = 7             |
| Length of main beams                                         | R = 55-$^5$/$_8$ <br> L = 59-$^5$/$_8$ | R = 55-$^3$/$_8$ <br> L = 58-$^3$/$_8$ |
| Circumference at smallest place between first and second points | R = 12-$^1$/$_8$ <br> L = 11-$^2$/$_8$ | R = 13-$^5$/$_8$ <br> L = 13 |

The bottom line for the Horn Hut rack, according to the unofficial score sheet, was 414-$^6$/$_8$ typical points. If accurate, I reflected, that would make it the number six typical elk in the world. When I mumbled words to that effect to George, he told me that he and his brother Hugh, co-owners of the heirloom rack, were aware of this, but weren't sufficiently interested in the dubious recognition granted by a sixth-place trophy-book listing to go to the trouble of having the head officially measured and entered.

Toward this attitude I had mixed emotions. I applauded the lack of ego suggested by the Carpenter brothers' marginal interest in the trophy books. But then, as a way-gone antler nut, particularly as regards elk, I would definitely have liked to see this one-of-a-kind rack officially scored.

Back home, the Horn Hut rack still very much on my mind, I phoned Alexandria, Virginia, and spoke with the Boone and Crockett Club's director of big game records. After all was said, I calculated that, with adjustments to convert the typical score to nontypical, the Horn Hut head would go 434 flat, tentatively making it the number two nontypical elk in the world.

When I phoned to inform George of this, he agreed that owning a bona fide number-two B&C head would be just fine. So why, I asked, hadn't he already had the rack officially scored and entered in the nontypical category? Because, he countered, until just then, he hadn't known that B&C even had a nontypical category for elk. (In point of fact, until 1986 it didn't.)

Elated by this turn of events, I recruited a photographer friend and repeated the 125-mile drive over the Continental Divide to Creede. While my friend was busy with his cameras, I asked George to recount for me the big rack's history. He began with a disclaimer.

"Five generations of Carpenters have lived in Colorado," he said, "and the head has been in the family all five of those generations. But even so, its history consists of little more than hearsay and speculation."

The head is very old, George explained, although no one can say exactly how old. Further, no hard evidence has ever turned up to suggest its origin—save for a vintage photograph dated 1910 that shows the distinctive mount hanging near the back of the crowded trophy room of the Cebolla Sportsman's Lodge . . . which was built and for many years operated by J.J. Carpenter, George's great grandfather.

It was probably, though not certainly, great grandfather Carpenter, long a hunter and hunting guide, who had killed the big bull—at the least, it seems certain that he was the first Carpenter to possess it. This could have been as early as the 1880s or as late as 1900. The most likely home of the big elk would have been upper Red Creek, which empties into the Gunnison River near Cebolla and, interestingly, is less than twenty crow-flight miles from the Dark Canyon of Anthracite Creek—one-time stamping grounds of the John Plute bull.

Tattered and obviously aged, the present cape (the skin of a big game animal's head, neck and shoulders, which a taxidermist stretches over a synthetic form to make a lifelike "full head mount") is known to have been with the rack at least since 1937, and George confided to me his personal belief that it was taken from the very bull that had grown the antlers.

"But," he cautioned, "I can't be certain of that, any more than I can say for sure who killed the bull, or where or when."

After a moment he added, "What's more, the antlers are a little loose, suggesting a cracked skull or maybe worse. I've often been tempted to split the cape to find out what's beneath; maybe it would clear up some of the mystery and confusion. But it's family property and I'd hate to damage it."

By this time I was itching to have the head officially measured, and asked George if I could arrange it. He agreed.

Then one evening the phone rang. It was George Carpenter.

"Dave," he said, the tone of his voice making me uneasy, "before you went to any more effort toward having my elk officially measured, I wanted to find out one way or another about those loose antlers. So I used a metal detector to see if there might be any wire or pins in the head, which would indicate that something is fishy. When the detector sounded off, I cut into the cape."

"Is the skull intact?" I asked, worried that a cracked and patched skull might disqualify the antlers for B&C consideration.

"Worse," George said. "There *is* no skull."

The disappointment was palpable in his voice.

"Just plaster . . . cast antlers mounted in a plaster skull."

End of big antler story two.

But not all was lost. Far from it.

So what if the bull that grew this magnificent rack of antlers had been cagey enough or lucky enough to live to shed them rather than falling to a bullet and having them sawn from his corpse? So what if J.J. Carpenter had found the shed antlers and admired them sufficiently to spring for a full head mount?

So what?

So it makes them ineligible for trophy-book honors, that's all. The rack's greatest value is its aesthetic value—the sheer joy of viewing and pondering it—and that remains wholly undiminished. Pick-ups or no, the Horn Hut antlers are a great rare treasure, among the grandest "horns" ever grown by any elk, anytime, anywhere. Should you ever be fortunate enough to see them, hold on to your socks.

# ❧ VII.

## THE "HORN" TRADE
### *The Good, the Bad, the Misunderstood*

> Elk have been growing and shedding antlers for
> thousands of years, and it seems that man has been
> infatuated with them for almost as long.
>
> —GARY WOLFE
> from *Bugle*

PERCHED ON THE WINDOWSILLS and hanging from the pine-plank
walls of my little mountain cabin are antlers representing all
four genera of North American cervids, and then some—mule
deer, whitetail, Rocky Mountain elk, Alaska-Yukon moose,
Shiras moose, barren ground caribou.

These include attached pairs, matched cast pairs, individual
cast-offs, sawn-off burrs and various other parts. With a single
exception, none are from animals I have killed myself. Some I
picked up during backcountry hikes or robbed from the
corpses of highway road kills; others were gifts from friends
who bagged them in such unromantic environs as flea markets
and garage sales. Their origins don't matter so much to me;
they aren't trophies; it's simply their forms I fancy. Even so,
disregarding relative beauty, the favorites among my modest
rack collection are those I found myself.

The antler hunt: It's become a ritual for me these past few
years, an invigorating springtime tonic, to stroll the local
Colorado conifer and aspen woods and to hike nearby Utah
and New Mexico's sandstone canyons in search of antlers
discarded by overwintering elk and mule deer.

But since cast antlers are even more elusive than the animals that shed them, my rack hunting has been, until recently, little more than a good excuse to get outdoors and shake off the winter blues, burn off excess winter-banked calories. In my first several years of searching, I managed to turn up only a few specimens worth bringing home, and most of these were sun-bleached and rodent-chewed: from elk, a couple (not a matched pair) of spikes, one of them with mild palmation and the beginnings of a fork at its tip; from mule deer, a small two-pointer and a larger forker with the tip of one tine broken and mended to resemble the head and neck of a swan, a slender three-pointer stained red from the Utah soil on which it long had rested, and a smallish four-pointer.

This past spring, however, rather than simply wandering willy-nilly through the woods hoping to luck into a cast antler, as I had always done before, I decided to inject some method into my meanderings.

Beginning in early March, I went afield on snowshoes to pinpoint the favorite haunts of our local overwintering elk. Tracks, trails, browsed plants, bark-chewed aspens, "drop zones" (where a loose cluster of hot-from-the-oven, acornlike pellet droppings melt a mosaic of marble-sized pits several inches down into the snow), the big, tublike depressions where the animals have lain and melted out the snow with their body warmth, the infamous yellow snow—these are among the spoor of elk in winter. It was to the richest of such places that I returned in early May, when the snow had gone and the bulls had cast their previous season's antlers. Somewhere.

It seemed like a sensible plan, this scouting and scheming. Yet, rather than antlers, when I arrived at the place I had thought might be a happy anlter hunting ground, I found only the bad news of some bits of bone, shreds of hide and patches of hair from a winterkilled elk calf—and a recently and well-used game trail leading to . . . who knew where? I decided to follow and find out.

A couple of miles up the mountain, at the top of a small, steep rise and just a few yards off the game trail, I spotted a single long, white tine protruding from the forest duff. When I cleared away the leaves and other ground debris surrounding the upthrust bone, I discovered this wasn't just another spike antler, but the tip of a long, heavy beam. And from that beam, lying unobtrusively low to the ground, projected brow (first), bez (second), trez (third), dagger (fourth; this one broken roughly off a couple of inches from its tip), fifth and royal (sixth) tines. I was looking at a battle-scarred six-point Rocky Mountain elk antler. The classic model.

After examining and admiring my prize for a few moments—it came from the animal's right side and had been daintily nibbled at by rodents, but otherwise was un-damaged—I began casting about in search of its mate. This I found straightaway, just a few yards on, lying tines-down and almost completely hidden beneath the leaf litter. This antler, however, had but a small, shark-tooth projection where the fifth tine should have been, thus qualifying as only a five-pointer. (According to Boone and Crockett rules, in order to qualify as a tine, an antler point must be at least one inch long, and longer than its base is wide.) I had found a dandy six-by-five.

Jubilant, I thrust the two big beams aloft, one in each hand, and whooped like an idiot. Or a football fan. With an antler over each shoulder, a triumphant smile on my face (Carolyn later would call the lasting expression a "poop-eating grin"), I turned back down the mountain—a successful hunter headed home with his bag.

Later, I put a steel tape to the pair. The six-point beam measured forty-one inches (1.04 meter) long, its five-point mate not quite forty inches (1.02m). The brow tines of both were just under a foot (thirty centimeters) in length; small fish by record-book standards, perhaps, but a big, beautiful, wondrous rack just the same—my first "trophy-quality" find after years on the antler trail.

I relate this insignificant anecdote for a reason: to illustrate the fascination that antler hunting and collecting hold—not just for reclusive, misanthropic old mountain goats like me— but for a great many folk, rural, urban and suburban, most of them quite normal. In fact, my own rack quests are mere play compared to the effort and expense expended by many antler aficionados eager to invest not just time and energy, but small fortunes in their search for blue-ribbon cast antlers.

In response to this growing enthusiasm, the Rocky Mountain Elk Foundation has recently inaugurated a program to score and record cast elk antlers found by its members— which, because they are no longer attached to a skull, are overlooked by Boone and Crockett, Pope and Young and the other trophy-book keepers, no matter how exceptional they may be.

But the hottest antler-hunting action of all takes place—not out in the woods, but in the big-little Wyoming tourist community of Jackson. On the third Sunday each May every year, scores of antler nuts rendezvous near the National Elk Refuge in Jackson Hole to take part in the world's largest public antler auction. The sale they have come to watch or participate in, however, is but the culmination of a months-long process of gathering, pairing, grading and bundling of elk antlers—an event known officially as the Elk Antler Project.

The project kicks off each spring as soon as the winter population of an average 7,500 elk have abandoned the refuge for their summering grounds in Grand Teton and Yellowstone national parks and on the Bridger-Teton National Forest. It is then that a human net of Boy Scouts and their adult supervisors fan out across the 24,700 acres of the preserve to collect the bounty of recently cast antlers.

(A sidenote: You may have heard that the calcium and other minerals found in cast antlers provide an important source of nutrition for rodents, and that collecting antlers thus endangers these small creatures. This simply is not the case. The several wildlife biologists to whom I put this question replied almost as one that while cast-offs make nice *bonuses* for the rodents that find and gnaw on them, antlers are not an essential part of the food chain. In fact, discounting the unusually bountiful situation at the National Elk Refuge, cast antlers are so relatively rare and widely scattered that the overwhelming majority of rodents live their entire lives without encountering a single one. Therefore, except in areas such as preserves and national parks where the activity is prohibited by law, there's no need to feel guilty about picking up cast antlers.)

Using the spring of 1988 as a typical example, 162 scouts and eighty-eight adults spent a collective 1,262 hours picking up a whopping 6,122 pounds (2,783 kilos) of elk antler. Conservatively figuring an average weight of five pounds per beam (which range from spindly spikes to massive six-by-six's and bigger), that's some 1,224 antlers. Come sale day, a boisterous crowd of about five hundred, of whom seventy-five were registered bidders, gathered at Jackson's town-square park to spend a total of $46,619 for those discarded headbones. That figures out to $7.62 per pound. (As of winter 1990–91, the current going rate for dry—that is, cast, as opposed to green, or velvet—antler is eight to twelve dollars a pound.)

Pushing up the average ante at these sales are the incredibly high bids some participants offer for trophy-quality matched pairs. In 1988, one bidder paid $1,950 for a spectacular six-by-six rack, outshining the *combined* two record sales from previous years of a thousand and nine hundred bucks. Additionally, there were (and are each year) several other multi-hundred-dollar sales of "book quality" or unique nontypical matched antler pairs.

Of the $46,619 take for 1988, $35,305 was returned to the refuge in the form of elk feed, to be used the following winter. The rest went to finance local Boy Scout projects. A good arrangement all around.

In addition to raising money to help feed the elk, a second reason for staging the annual antler project, in the words of assistant refuge manager Jim Griffin, is "to remove a tremendous temptation to thieves." If the antlers were allowed to lie around the refuge uncollected, pirates and profiteers would proliferate, frightening, stampeding and endangering the health of the winter-stressed animals. Thus, the annual Elk Antler Project is not just a fund-raiser, it's also effective in helping to protect the elk.

Even so, there are those who trespass onto the refuge in late winter to pilfer antlers virtually the moment they're cast, weeks before the Boy Scouts come around. Jim Griffin—who, like most refuge personnel, shares in the monumental task of law enforcement—describes a typical scenario of watching through binoculars as would-be thieves cruise the boundaries of the preserve in vehicles, stopping here and there to survey the terrain with spotting scopes, marking on topo maps the locations of prime cast antlers. After dark, these scheming scoundrels return to collect the best racks . . . only to be greeted by Griffin or a fellow enforcement officer when they arrive with their booty back at the road.

Why are people willing to break the law and risk their freedom (some, caught and convicted, have gone to prison) to try and make off with a few armfuls of elk antler? In most cases, it's not because they appreciate the aesthetics of cervid headgear. Rather, it's simple greed (or, occasionally perhaps, extreme need).

At the current average market price of ten dollars per pound for dry antler, that middling six-by-five pair I found up my local mountain last spring is worth better than a C-note. (Together, the two beams weigh nearly twelve pounds). A lone sneak thief could easily snatch up and walk off with several—perhaps half a dozen or more—such pairs *in a single foray* onto the National Elk Refuge in late winter. And antler pirates seldom work alone.

That's big money come easy, even should the hot antlers be fenced at a discount, as most are. Nice matched pairs, as we have seen, can be worth a small fortune. And the value of even run-of-the-mill cast antlers increases greatly when converted into jewelry and other decorative items.

Among the many popular items of antler jewelry and orna-
ments—often scrimshawed, occasionally carved, sometimes
inlaid with silver or turquoise, usually polished with jeweler's
rouge to resemble fine ivory—are belt buckles, bolo ties,
buttons, cribbage boards, earrings, knife handles, necklace
pendants, pipe stems and bowls, and handgun grips. A finely
crafted and scrimshawed belt buckle made from a big gnarly
elk or moose antler burr inlaid with silver, for example, can
fetch hundreds of dollars in a trendy western resort-town
tourist shop, with the remainder of the antler left over to
transform into dozens more, albeit somewhat less spectacular,
jewelry items.

The antler art industry notwithstanding, the major economic
value of antlers, the *really big* money, is to be found in the
so-called "horn trade." At the annual Jackson auction, after the
best matched pairs have been sold to high-rollers, the bulk of
the remaining lot—tens of thousands of dollars worth of ho-
hum cast antler—is sold to a relative handful of buyers serving
an antler-hungry oriental folk-medicine market. But even this
is small-time stuff compared to the *velvet* antler industry—the
*real* horn trade.

In his mid-fifties, Lou Wyman is pretty much what decades of
cowboy movies have conditioned us to expect an authentic
western rancher to be—independent, outspoken, even rug-
gedly handsome in a Clark Gable sort of way.

Likewise, the Wyman Ranch—ten thousand acres of lightly
timbered Rocky Mountain foothill country perched at seven
thousand feet in northwestern Colorado—perfectly satisfies
popular notions of how a working western ranch should look.
Its entrance gate is located miles from the nearest paved road.
The rambling ranch house is furnished with age-darkened
antiques. Off a ways, a huge barn with hayloft, its roof sagging
with the memories of decades of heavy snows, stands like a
tattered monument to the Old West. Beyond the barn squats a
low log bunkhouse, its rustic interior decorated with hunting

trophies and warmed by a cavernous stone fireplace. Completing the scene is a bucolic assortment of corrals, loading ramps, narrowing chutes, squeezes and sundry outbuildings, all Wyman-built from locally felled logs and home-milled lumber.

In fact, about the only thing missing from this otherwise classic western American Gothic is a lazing herd of lowing cattle. That's because Lou and Paula Wyman ranch critters a lot more interesting and aesthetic than a bunch of stinking, gut-bulged, dung-smeared, drool-dripping beeves; the Wyman ranch supports, depending on the season, from two hundred to 350 head of wapiti.

Wyman maintains his elk in three separate herds. The first group consists of sixty or so head kept pastured near the ranch house. These animals are about as close to domesticated as elk ever are likely to become. When Wyman herds his dilapidated flatbed truck out across the big white pasture early each winter morning to distribute the daily supplemental ration of alfalfa or grass hay, these pampered "backyard" wapiti fall in behind the motorized feed wagon as obediently as a platoon of boot-camp recruits queuing up at the chow hall.

The second herd, pastured farther afield, is wilder, has the run of a good deal more acreage, receives no supplemental feed in winter and will line out for yon side of the brushy hills at the slightest provocation. The third and largest herd—over a hundred adult animals plus their offspring—enjoys close to a thousand rolling, aspen-timbered acres across which to roam and graze, and is, in a practical sense, wild.

In addition to wholesaling fresh, organically grown elk meat to a major East Coast restaurant supplier, and distributing their own (Wyman Elk Ranch) brand of preservative-free elk jerky, the Wymans have developed a marketing strategy that includes selling live animals to zoos and other elk ranchers, housing and guiding a few paying shooters (I can't call them hunters) each fall and helping to satisfy the oriental craving for tonics and elixirs derived from velvet antler—the horn trade.

The use of antlers in various folk medicines is an Oriental tradition, dating back in China at least to the Han Dynasty, some two thousand years ago. Today, many oriental cultures—Korea, China and Tibet in particular—still rely heavily on folk remedies, turning to modern medicine, when available at all, only as a last resort. And among the most precious of these folk cures are the wide-ranging potions made from antler. Included in the oriental antler pharmacopoeia are prescriptions to combat anemia, apoplexy, bladder stones, bleeding, convulsions, deafness, epilepsy, fatigue, gout, heart trouble, headache, hypertension, insomnia, nervous disorders, rheumatism, snake bite, spermatorrhea, ulcers, vaginal hemorrhaging and, as they say, much much more.

Somewhat surprisingly, laboratory studies by both American and oriental researchers (the latter primarily at Kyung Hee University in Seoul) have shown that some antler preparations apparently live up to their folk reputations. Critics of these studies, however, point out that some experiments showing positive outcomes have not been properly controlled, while the results of failed experiments have a tendency to be brushed under the rug rather than publicized (as is true not just for science, but in all walks of life).

No real matter either way, probably, for, as Brown University's Richard J. Goss so aptly laid it out in his excellent text, *Deer Antlers* (Academic Press, 1983): "It is convenient if the beliefs of mankind are supported by scientific evidence. Lacking this, they seem to go on being believed anyway."

While antler from just about any cervid species will do for some budget-priced elixers, *elk* antler is demanded by the discerning, with North American *velvet* elk antler considered the Mercedes of the horn trade. This perception of North American excellence, together with the fact that the major consumer countries all suffer a severe shortage of wapiti, conspire to make the U.S. a leading supplier of antler to the Orient.

Some observers object to the horn trade on the grounds that it seems cruel to rob male cervids of the headgear natural selection has invested so many millions of years in providing, or simply on the grounds that private individuals have no business owning and dealing in wild animals. Other detractors point out that the velvet antler market earns for some of its workers the wages of sin, that potentially huge profits encourage rack poaching, or "horning"—the illegal killing of bull elk in early summer merely for their antlers. Unfortunately, there is some truth in each of these charges.

According to John Rice, Executive Director of the North American Elk Breeders Association (NAEBA), the current market value of velvet elk antler is fifty to eighty-five dollars per pound (winter 1990–91), depending on quality. (Among other things, buyers are looking for soft, porous, blood-filled cores to indicate a lack of ossification, or hardening.) Given that the head of an average adult bull elk is adorned with ten to fifteen pounds (4.5 to 6.8 kilograms) of the valuable bone. That ciphers out to a per-bull take of between five hundred bucks on the low end and $1,275 or more at the top. With little more work involved for a poacher than some walking, the squeeze of a rifle trigger, a few dozen strokes with a bone saw. Quite the temptation for men without scruples.

Fortunately, due to the workings of supply and demand, the poaching of velvet antlers for the oriental market isn't as great a problem today as it was back in the late 1970s, when bootleg velvet elk antler was going for $150 a pound.

Nor does the problem of horning compare with the blight of "head hunting"—poaching to supply the federally felonious yet brisk and growing black market trade in Boone and Crockett-quality horns and antlers . . . which sad fact prompts me to step to the pulpit for a brief sidetrack sermon.

It is documented fact, to mention a couple of examples, that a full-curl bighorn sheep head—horns, skull and cape—can bring in excess of ten thousand dollars in the trophy black market, while a "book quality" Rocky Mountain elk head can earn for its poacher a fee more in the neighborhood of twenty grand. Who, other than the poachers, is at fault here, and what can be done about it?

The Boone and Crockett Club is a venerable organization with a long and honorable tradition of promoting both wildlife conservation and hunter ethics. Even so, it is undeniable that Boone and Crockett's very existence, together with a couple of similar but smaller organizations, inadvertently promotes a multitude of ego-related hunting sins. Were all of these groups to shut down tomorrow and close the pages of their record books forever, the super-lucrative market for illegal trophy heads would disappear virtually overnight. Additionally, many of those unsporting albeit essentially law-abiding sports who now hunt for all the wrong reasons would either drop their expensive trophy pursuits in favor of something more competitive, offering more ego-gratification, or readjust their hunting attitudes for the better.

Worse though than a few insecure fat cats who use lots of money to compensate for their general lack of skill and personal fortitude in pursuing trophy-book recognition—far worse—are those scumsuckers who buy their "trophies" outright, thus fostering the black market trade in poached antlers and horns.

Of course, a general disbandment of trophy hunting clubs isn't likely to come about. Nor do I suggest it should. Still, for the improvement of hunting and its public image, for the protection of our wildlife resource, for the clubs' own good, Boone and Crockett and its spin-off organizations would be well advised to recognize forthwith and address more forcibly than it yet has the many and various problems inherent to their very existence. (If you don't take care of it yourselves, boys, someone else, sooner or later, is bound to step in and try to take care of it for you.)

So great is the profit potential in illegal head hunting that large professional crime rings often develop, their members employing such modern and expensive technologies as helicopters and police-band radios. It's nothing for a hit-team of poachers to gun down an entire herd of animals from a distance, then furtively approach to see if any of the corpses have heads worth the taking. The number and sophistication of tricks these professional criminals have devised to evade detection, capture and conviction is legend among wildlife law enforcement officers.

Meanwhile, the task of patrolling and protecting the sprawling 2.2-million-acre Yellowstone backcountry, where many of the worst such offenses haven traditionally been committed, is assigned to less than a score of wilderness rangers who don't usually work at night, when they're most needed, and who rarely enjoy the pricey benefit of aviation support.

But to return now to the subject at hand . . . none of this talk of unsporting and illegal trophy head-hunting alters the veracity of the charge that the oriental horn trade precipitates criminal activity. Velvet-antler poaching for this market long has been, and remains, a nagging problem in and around some elk-rich preserves and national parks, particularly poor old beleaguered Yellowstone.

There, in the oldest of our national parks, four to five antler poaching cases are brought to trial each year, the poachers having been nabbed by backcountry ranger patrols. Most poaching suspects are charged with federal felonies under the Lacey Act, with conviction bringing penalties as high as twenty thousand dollars in fines and up to ten years in federal prison, plus forfeiture of all personal property used in conjunction with the crimes—truck, airplanes, rifles and such. Yet more than a few desperadoes risk it every year.

The typical pattern is for a small team of "horners" to slip into a border area of a park or preserve's backcountry in late spring, gun down a number of bull elk in late evening or at night using spotlights, take only the velvet antlers and make their escape in the dark.

Lately, however, a few horners have become somewhat more sophisticated and, it must be grudgingly admitted, a bit less brutal. Instead of killing their quarry outright, some have taken to darting elk with tranquilizer guns, then amputating the antlers while the bulls lie incapacitated. No sooner are the racks removed than the victims wake and go their bareheaded ways—though certainly some worse for the wear, having been uncrowned and disarmed for the approaching rut and, since the antler stubs are left unsealed, losing a lot of blood in the process. Even so, most darting victims apparently survive, though a few such dehorned bulls subsequently are mistakenly killed when they wander out of the park and are shot by legal hunters carrying cow elk licenses.

Elk rancher Lou Wyman has given a lot of thought to the many criticisms lodged against the horn trade and, by association, against him. But the Wyman Elk Ranch, like an ever-increasing number of similar operations throughout the country, is a legitimate, state-licensed business, which, Lou feels, significantly *reduces* horn poaching by helping to sate the hungry market with legal velvet antler. Neither does Wyman feel guilty for robbing about half of his mature bulls of their racks each year.

When the time arrives to harvest velvet antlers, always before the late-June summer solstice, Wyman stages a wapiti roundup, herding selected bulls—mostly from his backyard herd— into a corral that vents into a narrowing chute leading in turn to a cattle squeeze modified especially for handling elk. When a bull enters the V-shaped squeeze, a gate drops down at the rear, preventing the animal from backing out. Simultaneously, the floor drops out so that the wapiti's body is squeezed by its own weight (thus the contraption's name) down into the tapered box and lodged there gently but firmly. Finally, the bull's head is immobilized in a snug collar so that the antlers can be sawn off without fear of the animal thrashing about and harming either itself or Wyman.

The instant the antlers are off, Wyman caps the stumps with paraffin to stanch bleeding, prevent infection and provide protection against injury until the wounds scab over and toughen (which takes only a few days). And since bull elk are compelled by instinct to spar before and during the fall rut, with or without antlers, Wyman usually leaves the brow tines—those two lower, downward-slanting points—in place as eye and face protection.

The "dehorning" operation takes but a few minutes per animal and, Wyman maintains, causes the bulls little if any pain. The rancher bases this hopeful assumption on the fact that elk are highly vocal creatures that don't hesitate to cry out when frightened or hurt, and no bull he has dehorned has ever uttered a sound, during or after the rapid surgery. Even back when he didn't use anesthetics.

Critics of this practice, however, point out that velvet antlers are highly innervated and their amputation, therefore, must be painful. Consequently, these days Lou Wyman, like most other modern elk ranchers, uses both sedatives and local anesthetics. The typical regime is to administer—or, better, to have a qualified vet administer—approximately 250 milligrams of Rompun or a Rompun-Ketamine blend per four hundred pounds of elk body weight to sedate the bull before two precision injections of local anesthetic are given at the base of each antler. Next, a tourniquet is applied to the pedicle at the base of each antler. Now, using a hacksaw or similar instrument, the antlers are removed.

The moment the antlers are off, they're inverted to prevent blood loss (the oriental trade demands blood-rich velvet antlers), wrapped and placed in a freezer.

Before the tourniquets are removed and an antidote (often Yohimbine) is administered to the sedated bull, many ranchers use this handy opportunity to administer any necessary vaccinations. Once the raw antler stubs are medicated and capped with wax, the bull is aroused and released, only temporarily worse for the wear.

The valuable commodity the captive bull has produced, meanwhile, is generally sold to an antler trader forthwith. Once the velvet antler reaches its destination, it is processed into various final products.

According to an article by Dr. J.C. Haigh, MRCVS, of the University of Saskatchewan, which appeared in the premiere

edition of the *NAEBA News* (the journal of the North American
Elk Breeder's Association) . . .

> The antler is prepared in at least three
> different ways. The softest part, where most of
> the blood is situated, is used for the production
> of an elixir. The middle part is cut wafer thin,
> and a powder is prepared from that portion of
> the antler near the base, which is the hardest.
> Fully hardened antler is also sold in Korea.
> This comes in the form of sections about 10cm
> long that are shaved very fine and added to
> water as a sort of soup.

Lou Wyman's business partner in the horn trade is Kern
Chung, a Korean-born engineer, chemist and export
entrepreneur now living in Colorado. I wanted to speak with
this man—to get the scoop on the oriental horn trade directly
from the mouth of an oriental horn trader. I was determined to
make the effort, but didn't know what response to expect,
since I'd heard rumors to the effect that oriental antler buyers,
having taken so much flak from various quarters (often for
good reason), tend to be taciturn.

Some may in fact be. But when I telephoned Mr. Chung, I
found myself speaking with an intelligent, educated, open
man of bright good humor. Although he spoke with a heavy
accent, Chung's English was infinitely superior to my Korean.
After a bit of introductory conversation, I presented the one
big query that contained all my smaller questions. "Tell me," I
said, "about the oriental horn trade." And he did, freely and,
nearly as I can determine, fully.

In prelude, Kern Chung emphasized that he deals only with
legitimate antler suppliers such as Lou Wyman. Having been
approached by what he believes were undercover U.S.
wildlife agents who attempted to sell him illegal velvet antler
at a tempting price (he wisely declined the offer), Chung is
acutely aware that oriental horn dealers are generally
regarded with no small suspicion, and feels that to buy from

illegal sources—such as the sneak-thieves of Jackson Hole or the horn poachers of Yellowstone—would be not only immoral and felonious, but incredibly stupid as well. (Some horn traders, unfortunately, have proven themselves to be all three.)

Chung went on to explain that while New Zealand, with its profusion of red deer ranches, is the leading producer of velvet antler in the free world, its product nonetheless has lately fallen out of favor with the oriental market, of which Korea accounts for some eighty percent. This is in large part because the aforementioned studies done in South Korea, under the direction of one Dr. Lee Sang In, have shown that antler produced by animals inhabiting New Zealand and other warm areas is pharmaceutically inferior to antler grown in cooler climates.

While all four North American cervid types have populations living in geographic areas that are cool or cold all or part of the year, the velvet antler of Rocky Mountain elk has become the uncontested star of the industry. And since velvet elk antler can be legally obtained only from privately owned animals, (or, rarely and only in small quantities, through other government-authorized channels), the produce of elk ranchers such as Lou Wyman is in great demand.

A second factor working in favor of North American elk antler is nutrition. While New Zealand's red deer (classified, I'm sure you recall, as conspecific with the wapiti) are restricted in pasturage and fed a monotonous supplemental domestic diet, only Wyman's backyard "feeder" herd is fed supplementally, and then only in winter. The rest of his elk have free run of a vast natural area providing a varied abundance of native food types—a dietary diversity that, Korean research has shown, produces antler abundantly rich in protein and important minerals.

From the Wyman Elk Ranch in Colorado to the consumer in Korea, China, Tibet or elsewhere, the per-pound price of antler increases—due to the commissions taken by various middlemen plus steep export tariffs—exponentially. As of

1989, the U.S. export duty on velvet antler was five hundred dollars per kilogram (2.2 pounds). The USSR, also a large producer, was taxing its exports at a rate equivalent to $550 per kilogram. At a "mere" three hundred bucks per kilo, the government of New Zealand was trying, though seemingly not too hard, to keep its antler industry competitive.

Curious about the taste of antler, I recently sampled about a quarter teaspoonful of hardened antler in powdered form— the sawdust resulting from hacksawing the burr off a cast moose antler that I picked up on the Alaskan tundra. I can report that it tastes like . . . well, actually there was very little taste of any kind. If pressed, though, I guess I'd say that it had a taste and texture remotely resembling dried parmesan cheese. But still I was left wondering what *velvet* antler tastes like and whether or not (an even more intriguing curiosity) it in fact produces the claimed aphrodisiac effect.

And so it was, toward the conclusion of my interview with Kern Chung, that I asked, "What does *panty* taste like?" (*Panty*, by humorous linguistic coincidence, is the oriental word for velvet antler prepared as an aphrodisiac.)

He laughed and said, "Oh, not so bad. A little like rare elk steak."

I then suggested that he send me—for research purposes, you understand—a few of the thin wafers into which *panty* is sliced, or a pinch of the powder into which it is ground after being carefully dried.

Came another knowing chuckle from Chung. "It's used mostly by tired old men. Do you really need it?"

He had me by the ego. Hence, I dropped the ploy and am left yet to wonder.

# ANTLER GROWTH STAGES

Raw pedicles just after casting old antlers.

Antler buds quickly sprout from pedicles.

Antler growth can be as rapid as a half inch a day.

Nearly finished antlers, still in velvet.

Finished antlers— solid, dead bone.

# ❦ VIII.

## HOPEFUL MONSTERS
### *A Look at "Freak" Antlers*

If something can go wrong, it will.
—MURPHY'S LAW

OVER THE YEARS, I've collected a small private library containing some of the most enlightened discourses ever written on the natural history of antlers and the animals that wear them: books both scholarly and anecdotal, as well as stacks of scientific papers. Yet no one of these resources, nor even all of them together, fully explains the mysteries of why and how deer grow nontypical (commonly and often not without reason referred to as "freak") antlers. This void is not, of course, the fault of the authors and editors of these texts and papers. Considering how little is known with absolute certainty about the evolution, growth and functions of *normal* antlers, it would be a bit much to expect science to have answered all the even more convoluted questions about the abnormal.

Among the more common rack uncommonalities are antlered females, palmation in normally nonpalmate species (deer and elk), radical differences in size and shape between right and left beams, three or even four main beams rather than just two, and—the most common antler anomaly of all—extravagant numbers and shapes of extra or "supernumerary" tines. (Michael McCurdy's sublime cover woodcut, for a handy example, is based on a supernumerary-laden Idaho elk, the world's number six B&C nontypical.)

Of the latter, an example, lifted from the Boone and Crockett Club's *Records of North American Big Game,* eighth

133

edition: The largest total number of tines on record for a pair of typical whitetail antlers is twenty-three, while for nontypical whitetail it's forty-nine.

Even though far more remains murky than has so far been clarified, research into the causes of antler abnormalities is longstanding and ongoing, and knowledge is gradually being gained. The earliest informed discussion of the phenomenon of freak antlers I've yet turned up was written by Frank C. Clark for the July 24, 1916 issue of *California Fish & Game.* The article was later summarized by naturalist-hunter-wildlife artist E.T. Seton for inclusion in Volume III of his 1927 classic, *Lives of Game Animals.* It is from the Seton summary I quote, with editorial quaintnesses of the time maintained (I have, however, added occasional italics for emphasis):

Freak antlers may be the result of any of 4 causes:

1. *Violence* to the antlers themselves during their growth. These show as breaks healed up, like a broken limb, with a bony mass at the weld and the outer part usually at a wrong angle.
2. *Food shortage or overabundance* during the growth. Thin Deer always grow slender, undeveloped antlers; Deer from a range where good food abounds, are often excessively developed.
3. *Injury to the testicles,* which results in numberless strange phenomena unlike those produced in any other way; for the antlers are important sex characters.

   If the buck is castrated when young, the antlers, when grown, are small and deformed. If the animal be castrated when in the velvet, the antlers are never dropped, always remain in the velvet, and keep on slowly growing in odd shapes.

   If castration be performed when the antlers are hard and perfect, they are never dropped at all. It is not easy to say how castration may take place in a wild Deer. The testes are placed beyond the reach of ordinary injury. But there is the possibility of the animal descending on a sharp snag. Also, cold has been known to settle in the testicles, terminating in atrophy. There have been cases of Buffalo castrated by Wolves— which suggest several possibilities.

4. Any severe *injury to the body or bones* of
   the animal, while the antlers were growing. Nearly
   all injured bucks develop deformed antlers, and
   nearly all bucks with deformed antlers show an old
   wound. Furthermore, the malformation in the antlers
   is almost always on the same side as the injury,
   and in cases where both sides of the animal have
   sustained an injury, both antlers are usually deformed.

How do Frank Clark's "four causes" fare after three score
and more years of additional research? While not having
crossed the decades unscathed, these turn-of-the-century ob-
servations have nonetheless held up surprisingly well. Here's
a point-by-point comparison:

*Violence to the antlers themselves during growth.* The critical words here are *during growth*—that is, before hardening
and velvet shedding. At this stage, a fractured tip might droop
or dangle, loosely attached to the shaft by its natural velvet
sock. As blood carries minerals up through the shaft to fuse the
fracture, the broken portion mends in its skewed posture. I
have one such antler in my collection, its broken tip mended
exactly as Clark describes, "with a bony mass at the weld and
the outer part [projecting] at a wrong angle."

If, however, a break is so severe as to completely separate
an antler tip from its shaft, the tip will die, dropping off when
the velvet is shed. Or, a rarer possibility, if a growing antler tip
is cleanly amputated, velvet and all, the injured shaft may
regenerate a replacement for the part lost. The new tip, however, is likely to be misshapen and smaller than the original,
often looking something like a claw.

An extreme example of growth abnormality occurred when
one of the captive whitetail bucks at Dr. A.B. Bubenik's
Canadian research facility accidentally split its right beam
early in the annual growth cycle: Growth continued, and the
animal produced a more-or-less matched pair of gigantic,
ornately deformed antlers. But odder yet, this phenomenon
was repeated through the next several growth cycles, though
the size and shape of the succeeding racks differed each year.

The reason for this annual recurrence, Bubenik says, is that the injury damaged the pedicle, thus permanently affecting antler production.

Still, while such bizarre malformations as those of the Bubenik whitetail *can* result from injuries to velvet antlers, most such accidents cause only minor deformities in comparison to freaks arising from other causes.

*Food shortage or overabundance during antler growth:* While the observant Mr. Clark was not incorrect in saying that malnourished cervids grow small, slender antlers, and that well-fed animals grow larger racks, he was mistaken to have included nourishment or the lack thereof as a cause of *freak* antlers. Unusually small or large antlers with normal shape and symmetry are abnormal, but not true nontypicals.

Further, Clark's implication that quantity of food intake is the controlling antler-growth factor needs clarification. It isn't so much the *amount* of food that controls antler growth as it is the food's *quality,* measured primarily by calcium, phosphorus and protein (especially collagen) content. It's entirely possible for a cervid to get sufficient calories from its food to sustain a healthy, perhaps even plump body, but still be unable to produce a good rack because its diet is lacking in minerals essential to normal antler growth.

Conversely, a skinny, undernourished cervid is not likely to produce large, healthy antlers even if it somehow gets sufficient minerals in its scant diet (say, by regularly licking a livestock mineral block); for if it were getting enough protein to support normal antler growth, its body would never have withered. (You'll recall that antlers are luxury organs, meaning that they get fed only after those organs more essential to the animal's general well-being are satisfied.)

A final note on nutrition as it affects antler growth: Malnourishment in an adult cervid during a single antler-growth cycle will produce undersized antlers *only for that cycle,* while severe malnourishment in the crucial early months of life is likely to cause permanent stunting of body and antlers throughout the animal's career.

*Injury to the testicles:* Virtually everything Clark had to say on this point remains valid, although a great deal more is known today about the whys and wherefores. Because castration can easily be inflicted surgically and its effects closely monitored in captive cervids, a large—perhaps inordinately so—amount of research has been conducted in this area, often with astonishing (some would say horrifying) results.

Perhaps the most grotesque of antler deformities resulting from testicular injury or disease (or controlled experiment) manifests itself as a knobby mass of bone squatting low on the luckless animal's head and looking not unlike a misshapen honeycomb or an exposed brain. Overall, though, while a hormone imbalance caused by castration or testicular atrophy (shrinkage) due to accidental injury or, rarely, disease—a sad state referred to in the scientific lingo of hypogonadism—can and occasionally does lead to dramatic antler disfigurations (commonly referred to as "cactus bucks") the relative number of freak racks caused by hypogonadism in the wild is insignificant.

*Injury to the body or bones of an animal (excluding the antlers themselves) while the antlers are growing:* Biologists refer to this phenomenon—an injury or disease in one part of the body that interferes with the normal development or functioning of another part—as a "systemic" influence.

While it's true that a significant injury to, say, a hind leg, can and often does cause growing antlers to become deformed, Clark's 1916 assertion that the affected antler is "almost always on the same side as the injury" conflicts with the contemporary consensus that a systemically malformed antler is most often, though not always, contralateral, or occurring on the side *opposite* the injury. Further confusing things—and directly contradicting Clark—is the fact that many cervids receive severe bodily injuries yet produce normal antlers on both sides.

Overall, probably the most interesting and compelling discussion of antler abnormalities I've encountered came not from a book or research paper, but from conversation with the Rocky Mountain Elk Foundation's Dr. Gary Wolfe, former wildlife manager and biologist for Vermejo Park Ranch in New Mexico and Colorado.

Across Vermejo Park's seemingly endless expanse of prime big game habitat roam four to six thousand totally wild Rocky Mountain elk. For twelve years, Wolfe enjoyed a research biologist's dream in that he could daily observe wild elk and their behavior in a natural theater, then, come the annual hunting season, examine the antlers and carcasses of the wapiti killed by the paying hunters who visit the ranch each fall.

Wolfe's off-the-cuff estimate is that less than five percent of all mature bull elk at Vermejo Park ever develop abnormal antlers. But, interestingly, most of the freak antlers he did examine there resulted from a cause not listed among Clark and Seton's quartet of possibilities: It was not injury to growing antlers. It was not malnutrition. It was not accidental castration leading to hypogonadism. Nor was it systemic influence. Rather, the single major cause of malformed antlers at Vermejo Park during Gary Wolfe's long tenure there was pedicle injuries received during rutting battles between mature bulls with hard, dead, finished antlers.

When a sparring bull receives a particularly vicious blow to his antlers, the shock is translated down the main beam to the pedicle—which, you will recall, is a permanent bony protrusion of the skull itself. This sudden and severe trauma, in turn, can and does occasionally cause a stress fracture to open along the front and around the inner base of the pedicle, following lines of structural weakness in the skull.

Often, a bull injured in this way dies forthwith of cerebral concussion. But among those that survive to undergo the healing process, gravity encourages the weighty antler attached to the damaged pedicle to sag, pulling and holding the loosened pedicle away from the skull so that it mends at an eccentric angle. Come early spring, the old antlers drop off, with new growth sprouting from the pedicles almost immediately.

In this new growth cycle, the afflicted bull will have one antler developing normally, while the sad product of the injured pedicle wanders forward, down, then back up—or, more commonly, forward and down, and down, eventually growing beyond the end of the muzzle. From then on, each time the elk dips his head to nip a bite of grass, the soft, velvet-covered tip of the wayward beam will bang against the ground. Over the three to five months of antler growth, this rough treatment, repeated thousands of times, shapes a wildly deformed antler—a tineless, stunted shaft that rarely attains a length of more than twenty inches (fifty-one centimeters) and carries a grotesque club of eight to ten inches (twenty to twenty-five cm) in diameter at its end. Meanwhile, the antler on the uninjured side matures normally.

Another fairly common cause of antler deformities overlooked by Clark and Seton is disease. Technically, this is a systemic condition, but rather than leading to a malformed antler on only one side, disease most often causes more-or-less symmetric deformities of both antlers.

One particularly nasty disease occurring in elk that live in the warmer southern reaches of the species' North American range is the work of the internal parasite *Elaeophora schneideri* (often referred to as "brainworm"). The subadult form of this tiny roundworm, transported by the green-headed horsefly, invades a host animal's bloodstream when the fly inflicts its vicious bite. It then travels to and lodges in a carotid (neck) or cerebral (brain) artery where it continues to grow, eventually obstructing the flow of blood to the victim's brain.

The resulting condition, known in domestic sheep as "sorehead," manifests itself in symptoms including clear-eyed blindness, disorientation and necrosis (death and decaying) of the tips of muzzle, tongue and ears. Additionally, should the victim be a bull in velvet, the severely restricted blood supply can result in antlers that are, in Gary Wolfe's words, "stunted, gnarly and generally malformed."

Reflecting on other antler abnormalities observed during his time at Vermejo Park, Wolfe recalls having encountered only one antlered female elk. This cow was wearing soft, velvet-covered nubbins about two inches (five cm) long—at a time of year when normal antlers on bulls were hard and polished. In his postmortem examination, Wolfe could find nothing unusual about the antlered cow's sex organs; she was not a hermaphrodite.

The genetic potential to sprout stunted antlers exists in all species of female cervids and occurs most often (which isn't to say very often) among older, barren cows. Research suggests that the condition results when ovarian cysts prompt an abnormal production of androgens, or male sex hormones. To make antlers, however, this hormonal imbalance needs the help of a traumatic catalyst, such as an accidental head injury (does this phenomenon sound familiar?), to release the foreskull's latent antler-growth program. But since female cervids lack the facilities for production of the male hormone testosterone—necessary to harden and finish the antlers—the wimpy little growths, called "eo-antlers," never harden, shed their velvet or drop off (except in cases where they freeze and die).

Conversely, Wolfe found no antlerless mature bull elk, or "hummels," at Vermejo Park—an observation (or lack thereof) consistent with the rest of North America.

The story of the hummel, an abnormality that appears with some regularity among Eurasian red deer, is worth summarizing here as an interesting example of a nontypical mating strategy. While an immature, elderly or otherwise underqualified male—as signified by underdeveloped antlers—stands little or no chance of making off (or out) with a member of a dominant bull's harem, a hummel sometimes can manage to sneak into a harem and have his fun. This is possible exactly because, without antlers, he resembles a cow, thus failing to attract the attention of the busy herd bull. Why this strategy has evolved in the Eurasian version of *C. elaphus* but not in his North American conspecific, remains a delightful mystery.

"Among the more intriguing antler abnormalities I did observe at Vermejo Park," Dr. Wolfe recalls, "was the occasional adult bull, aged 2-1/2 years or older, having only two- or three-inch (5.1 to 7.6 cm) stubs for antlers. Considering their minimal length, the average circumference of these stubs, at six to eight inches (15.2 to 20.3 cm), was impressive. These were not the stumps of broken-off beams, but whole, hardened and polished antlers."

Wolfe examined the sex organs of each of the several "stub bulls" brought in by hunters over the years, even going so far as to send the excised testes to the University of New Mexico for microscopic examination in their histology (tissue structure) laboratory. No abnormalities were found.

After eliminating the other obvious possible causes—injury, disease, hormonal imbalance—Wolfe arrived at the conclusion that these remarkably consistent deformities must be genetic in origin and, thus, hereditary by nature. The fact that all of the stub bulls came from the same region of the ranch further strengthens this hypothesis.

This brings us to an important point concerning antler abnormalities in general, a point upon which both the 1916 writer Frank Clark and his esteemed 1927 editor Ernest Thompson Seton failed to comment: It is probable that the single most common cause of antler anomalies—both minor and bizarre—is *genetic mutation.*

Time after time, strikingly similar antler abnormalities appear among several members of a cervid population sharing a geographically described gene pool. Likewise, a distinct antler abnormality often occurs in several generations of members of the same gene pool. (For example, I have seen evidence of one such "freak pool" operating in a local mule deer population to produce beautifully ornate, supernumerary-studded, nontypical racks all somewhat similar in appearance.)

These circumstances strongly suggest the workings of heredity. This, of course, is believed to be the way antlers evolved in the first place . . . genetic mutations occurring at random—producing what evolutionary biologists have poetically referred to as "hopeful monsters"—then proving either useless or a liability and gradually dying out, as most do, or finding a use and so getting passed along from generation to generation, being reinforced and gradually refined in the process.

In an 1884 scientific journal, naturalist John Dean Caton described a Texas whitetail buck with heavily palmated, bilaterally symmetric antlers. Drawings of this animal show an antler configuration closely resembling that of the Eurasian fallow deer (*Dama dama*). In his discussion, Caton cautions that "mechanical injury" to the antlers cannot be ruled out as the cause of this deformity, but points out that the antlers' . . .

> bilateral symmetry, coupled with the fact that
> another animal with similar antlers had been
> sighted in the same region, strongly suggests
> that this unusual configuration might have been
> the result of genetic mutation. The implications
> for the evolution of palmate antlers in moose,
> reindeer, and fallow deer are obvious.

Just as the normal antlers of today were, in millennia past, genetic "freaks"—evolution's "hopeful monsters"—similar wild cards are in play today, insidiously influencing the shape of antlers yet to come.

*Afterthought*

# THE HUNTER AS NATURALIST
## *An Oxymoron?*

Fewer and fewer are those who can identify.
Greater and greater are the well-meaning but
ignorant who debase what I do as unnecessary
or unneeded, who criticize my personal, spiritual
activities as mere "sport." What part of their heritage,
I wonder, should I demand they do without?

—CRAIG MEDRED
in *Bugle*

IT SEEMS A SIN of omission to consider antlers and the animals that wear them at such length as we have in the preceding chapters without also taking a good hard look at the sister topic of hunting. Like yin and yang, deer and deer hunting are inseparable—so it is now, so it has been since the dawn of humanity. And so, many would argue, it should be.

Thus and therefore, I offer the following "afterthought," aimed primarily at nonhunters—that four-fifths majority of Americans who have no strong opinions one way or another.

I am a hunter. Not merely "a person who hunts," but someone to whom this ancient, natural and honorable activity is an essential and deeply meaningful part of life. As such, I take no small umbrage at the unfounded attacks of anti-hunters—or, on the other side of the philosophical coin, at the behavior of what too often passes for hunters these strange days, those

143

"Har har Joe let's grab a coupla six-pax an' hop on the ATV's an' go scare up sumpin' to shoot at" crowd.

When I speak kindly of the "hunter," I refer to the man or woman who stalks unobtrusively through forest and field or sits quietly alongside game trail or watering hole, and who eats what he or she shoots, whether meat is the primary motive for hunting or not. While I acknowledge the grunt-work and patience required to lure in and shoot a bear over a bait, I see no real challenge, no compassion, no sense of fair play and, ultimately, no point. As to shooting a hound-treed bear or lion: that's not hunting, it's hot-blooded execution.

Be all that as it may, during Colorado's monthlong archery season for deer and elk each fall, I become a hunting bum, pushing aside all else that's push-asidable in order to spend every possible moment—this year, as usual, it was about five hours an evening for thirty straight evenings—roaming the steep conifer and aspen forests that frame my mountain home. My primary goal at such times, though not my only goal, is to kill an elk or a mule deer. Maybe both. After a quarter-century of practice, I'm passably good at it.

For the remaining eleven months each year, I study wildlife and its habitat and do what I can to help protect both, giving of my time, money and ink. I like to think of myself not just as a hunter, but as a hunter-naturalist.

Is this a moral hypocrisy? Is the concept of hunter as naturalist (even amateur naturalist) an oxymoron, a contradiction in terms? Am I a liar and a fool for publicly professing to care a great deal about the welfare of wild animals, then turning around once a year and—not just hunting, but finding deep meaning and solace in the experience? To expand the question, were Teddy Roosevelt, George Bird Grinnell, Aldo Leopold, Ernest Thompson Seton, John James Audubon and others among our most important early naturalists and wildlife conservationists hypocrites because they, too, were hunters?

I think not. To the contrary, autobiographical accounts suggest it was hunting that first awakened in these men, as it would in me some decades later, a compelling love of nature and an insatiable curiosity concerning its workings.

Born in a large city, from earliest childhood I longed—almost instinctively, it would seem—for field and stream, river and lake, the mountains. In satisfying this chronic outdoor itch, my father—who worked twelve hours a day, six-and-a-half days a week keeping bread on the family table—was little able to help. Fortunately, there were other males in the family both qualified and, to varying degrees, willing to pinch-hit.

My maternal Uncle Charlie Harper was one. On rare but fondly remembered occasions Uncle Charlie would allow me to tag along after him, albeit unarmed, as he roamed the Oklahoma weed fields, his wirey pointer, Dick, ranging out ahead, nose working, tongue lolling almost to the ground, hot on the trail of bobwhite quail. And sometimes, back at home, Uncle Charlie would bring out a rifle or revolver or shotgun, lecture me briefly about safety around firearms, then allow me to handle the weapons, feel their forms, heft their weight, inhale the heady aromas of powder solvent and gun oil. Even more memorable, though, were Charlie Harper's tales of deer camps in Colorado, Wyoming or other points far west. I remember thinking, already dreaming, the *Rockies*.

But Uncle Charlie was too much like I would become as an adult—curmudgeonly, too jealous of his rationed time afield—to allow a skinny, burr-headed kid full of questions to slow him down more often than occasionally.

I fared some better with Harlis Harper, a country cousin. If I was ten at the time, Harlis was no more than twenty. Compared to Uncle Charlie, Harlis was a sucker for my take-me-hunting begs. On frequent Saturdays—arming me, as I learned to respect and handle firearms, first with a Daisy lever-cock BB gun, then a pump-piston pellet rifle and finally an old single-shot bolt-action .22—Harlis would lead out across grassy field and in amongst tangled hardwoods in search of game birds, squirrels, cottontails . . . and, as I would gradually become aware, something a lot bigger.

"There's more to hunting than just stomping around trying to scare up something to shoot at," I remember Harlis saying, almost as if to himself. "And there's a damnsight more to it than the killing."

Harlis' idea of hunting was the antithesis of thrashing around. Rather, we would walk slowly and quietly and stop often—standing still as statues, listening, looking, breathing in the clean country air—then move slowly on. And when we did spot a bird or an animal ahead, whether it was game or not, Harlis (and I by example) would stand for long moments, just watching.

Thus, gradually, were awakened in me the broader possibilities of hunter as observer, observer as appreciator, appreciator as student—in short, hunter as amateur naturalist. Over the years, across the decades, my concept of hunter as naturalist has matured, as have I.

What is he, who is he, this odd-duck hunter-naturalist character?

In my reckoning, the hunter-naturalist is a woodsman of the traditional persuasion. He knows and respects the natural world and enters it without fear. Instead of streamers of Day-Glo engineer's tape littering his trail to guide him safely home, he relies on map, compass, terrain features, the sun, the moon and stars, an attentive eye, memory, *himself*.

At home, the hunter-naturalist may or may not have trophies of the hunt decorating the walls of a woody den, but he is certain to have bookshelves filled with field guides—birds, mammals, trees, wildflowers—plus stacks of magazines both hook-and-bullet and natural history in content, photos, paintings, maybe a cast antler or similar token of good times abroad in nature.

Afield, the hunter-naturalist pays attention and consequently knows something of the meanings of the many and various wildlife vocalizations—territorial, all's-well, intraspecific squabbling, mild alarm, flat-out panic. He can recognize the rustling sound of a squirrel gamboling in dry leaves and the sharp, arboreal snap of a brittle branch breaking under the weight of that same squirrel or a clumsy bird. He knows the *chuck-chuck-chuck . . . thunk* of a liberated cone bouncing down through the limbs of a tall pine and coming home to earth. And he can tell each and all of these quite similar sounds from the hard, heavy *crack!* of a deer or an elk hoof crushing a fallen limb.

Further, the hunter-naturalist knows whether it is an elk or a deer (and in areas where both species of the latter abound, whether whitetail or muley) that has spooked and fled just ahead—knows just from the distinctive sounds each makes running. Likewise, he can tell the birdlike coalescence chirps of cow and calf wapiti from the similar but sharper bent-note calls of the red-shafted flicker and other woodpeckers.

While the hunter-naturalist values his hunting weapons as fine tools, he does not worship them as icons, nor does he consider ballistics charts as holy scripture, but reserves his true reverence for nature. He knows where local species of wildlife eat, drink and sleep, and when. He knows when they breed and when and where they give birth. He knows the influences upon elk and deer of full moon and approaching storm. He can follow a scant blood trail—by flashlight if necessary—and, more important, has the conviction to stay on it, come hail or high water, until the job is finished. He can read a cervid track for freshness, direction and speed of travel, and even, under favorable circumstances, wager an educated guess at the sex of the maker. And he may well prefer the wild, funky, barnyard scent of elk to any chemical potion man (or wo-man) has ever concocted.

The hunter-naturalist approaches hunting—not as just another form of competition for bragging rights, or, worse yet, as a way to bolster his insecure maleness—but as an invaluable learning experience, even a pilgrimage.

And all of this—the sights, the sounds, the smells, the reverence felt, the knowledge earned, the whole wild shebang—means a great deal to him (and, increasingly, to her), the hunter-naturalist.

Thus, Harlis Harper helped me to mature and to expand my life.

As soon as I was old enough to drive and had saved (and borrowed from my parents) enough to buy my first car, I took to going fishing and hunting on my own hook at every opportunity—the former oftentimes with like-minded friends, the latter more often than not alone.

I remember, on Fridays during deer season, driving forty-five miles after school to hunt whitetails for the remaining two hours until dark, my weapons an Osage orange longbow and a quiver of handmake cedar arrows, then crashing for the night in the cold, cramped backseat of my '53 Chevy with Okie coyotes yipping and yapping all around. Then up again before daylight to hunt all day Saturday. And Sunday. God but I loved it all, even the mild misery, as I do yet today.

It took me two years of hard trying to kill my first deer, a beautiful big November doe that walked beneath the oak limb upon which I was tenuously perched, shivering in my boots. My arrow split her heart and she died running five seconds later. I remember being simultaneously elated and saddened—an emotional conflict I have since come to know well, and which I often hear fellow hunters echo.

I am now middle-aged, and remain a bowhunter. While I'm not sure I would claim that bowhunting is somehow "better" than gun hunting, for me it has been infinitely more satisfying. I like things simple and slow and not too easy. (Otherwise, why bother?) But that's mere personal preference. In the end, it isn't the weapon that separates the slob from the serious hunter, but knowledge, skill and attitude. Attitude and the actions it determines.

That, I guess, explains why I'm so troubled by the culture- and advertising-induced trend among many nimrods these days—both riflemen and archers—to rely ever more heavily upon technology in a self-defeating effort to make hunting as easy and certain as possible. To me, this seems back-assward. To make my hunting as primitive, natural and challenging as possible, I vigorously eschew gadgetry. If some years I fail to fill the freezer because I can't get myself to within a few breath-holding yards of a deer or an elk and set up an un-obstructed shot, so be it; the weather is halcyon during the early bow season, the woods and wildlife undisturbed.

Come rifle season, my spirits soar to see—which I do most every year—a father and son or grandfather and grandchild or uncle and nephew afield together . . . moving slowly, talking in whispers if at all, the eager youngster emulating the sage elder's every move. Harlis and me.

What a contrast this is to those Day-Glo gangs of good old boys who roll into small western towns each October in forty-foot motor homes towing trailers stacked high with ice coolers and ATV's, hog up two or three spaces in the market parking lot, lumber out and trail into the store for a week's supply of groceries and—the essential red-neck lubricant—lots and lots of beer.

Typically, and sadly for them, few of these equipment-laden sports will ever venture far from where some variety of wheels can carry them. Most are poor physical specimens and sadly unskilled in woodsmanship. Consequently, they tend to be more of a threat to themselves, to the scenery (all that Day-Glo tape! all those empty beer cans!) and to other hunters than they are to the local wildlife, which can smell their breath a mile away.

But this condemnation applies only to a minor subspecies, not to the entire family of hunters. Most hunters, the "silent majority" if you will, are at least serious and conscionable if not downright reverential about their hunting. They are thoughtful predators playing a proper and important role in the natural scheme of things. It is, after all, the predators, human and otherwise, who have sculpted the incredible defenses of today's antlered species. Predator and prey; it's a quintessentially symbiotic relationship—as Darwin was among the first to recognize.

It's the old story: Those animals that are born with or some-how acquire physical features or behavioral traits that provide them with an advantage over others of their kind tend to live longer, breed more successfully and so pass on their genes (and, it might be argued by an ethologist, their learned be-haviors as well) more successfully than those less well adapted to their environment. In the face of this stiff competi-tion, those individuals and species less fit are squeezed out. Among prey species, the weak, sick, lame and lazy are preferred by predators (and for good reason: they're easier to catch and overpower) and so become the first, often the only, to go. Exactly as it should be.

"It is the wolves that keep the caribou strong."

Through this long slow winnowing process have evolved the most masterful self-defense organisms in the animal kingdom, the Cervidae. There is no better eye-ear-nose-reflex package going than the deer. To get to within striking range of a deer, a predator must understand and strive to defeat this remarkable animal's superb senses. This is the challenge of the serious hunter.

Take, for an insightful instance, vision.

Deer see differently than we do. Not necessarily better. Certainly not worse. Just differently. Your eyes are set side-by at the front of your head and more or less three inches apart pupil to pupil. This arrangement has each eye viewing an object from a slightly different angle, providing you (and most other predators) with binocular (two-eyed) vision. In its turn, binocular vision makes possible the precise depth perception so critical to the success of the hunter, human or otherwise; whether you're a mountain lion about to leap from a rocky ledge onto the back of a passing deer, or an archer aiming a bow at a wapiti bull, it's essential to have an accurate sense of the distance to your target. But there is a trade-off: The front-set arrangement of your eyes severely limits your peripheral, or side vision.

Since a major threat to deer and other prey species is the lurking possibility of predators sneaking in from the sides or rear, natural selection has positioned their eyes on opposite sides of their heads, giving them near wrap-around vision. But while this arrangement is ideal for defensive scanning, it precludes viewing an object simultaneously with both eyes, robbing deer of fine-tuned depth perception.

No great matter. Among prey species, visually determining the exact distance to something suspicious isn't nearly so important as knowing if, when and how that suspicious something moves. And the eyes of deer are privy to the slightest movement.

Too, there are those big, top-set ears that swivel like scanning radar to receive sounds in stereo, much as our eyes receive images, providing a sense of audio depth perception. If something within the deer's extremely wide field of vision moves, even slightly, the ever-alert animal will spot that movement. And if the mover makes any sound, such as a slight rustling of leaves, a cough, a fart, the deer's dish-antennae ears will provide an instant fix on the range. Between the two, far more often than not, the predator goes hungry.

But the finest and most important of the deer's defenses is its nose—virtually undefeatable unless the wind is constantly in the predator's favor, which situation cervids strive diligently to prevent by employing such clever tactics as bedding facing downwind in order to eyeball their fronts while their noses guard the rear.

This keen sensory triad—sight, sound and scent—makes the deer a most formidable challenge to the hunting archer who must get close in order to assure a clean kill. Most experienced bowhunters hold out for unobstructed shots of twenty-five yards or less. An expert rifleman with the right weapon, on the other hand, can kill a deer at two hundred yards or more. This disparity is not unlike the difference in war between a grunt fighting with a bayonet and a pilot dropping a bomb; the former an intensely personal act, the latter made impersonal by technology.

But gun hunting, too, is necessary in order to maintain balanced and healthy deer populations in this shrinking modern world. On our own, we archers could never get the job done—there simply are not enough of us, and our weapons are too limiting.

Either way, of course—bayonette or bomb—it's still killing, and a moral code is implied.

At the meat market recently, my attention was captured by a tank containing a dozen or so live lobsters. Their claws were bound with thick rubber bands, their world reduced to plastic, glass and a few gallons of stale gray water—waiting to be purchased, carted off and tossed (some say screaming) into a boiling pot.

From the lobster tank, my thoughts wandered to the slaughterhouse, to the poultry factory, to the fetid veal pen and various other grisly commercial operations that provide America with its meat.

Then I thought of hunting. By comparison, it's a natural and healthy arrangement—beneficial not only to the hunter but, arguably at least, to the hunted as well.

Of course, as the vegans—those hard-nosed vegetarians who shun not just meat, but all animal-derived products in any form (eggs, dairy products, leather)—are quick to point out and evangelical in the doing, the human body does not really need meat to survive and even prosper.

How true. In fact, for a couple of years back in the mid-'70s, while living on the West Coast, I became a something of a vegetarian myself (I ate cheese and eggs, which disqualified me from the ascetic ranks of veganism) and enjoyed excellent physical health. Being still young (compared at least to now), my "veggie" years in California, albeit perhaps coincidentally (how can I ever know for certain?) were the most physically fit of my life. I walked at least three miles a day, ran four more, swam in the cold Pacific, instructed at a weight-lifting gym, chased the girls and had energy left to spare.

Still, come mealtime, something vital always seemed to be—well, *missing*.

Then one evening shortly after moving to the rural Rockies, I was offered meat at the home of a friend. It was wild meat—

the cleanest, leanest, most healthful meat there is. She caught
me in the right mood—curious about RKV stew (road-killed
venison), which I had never before tried, and hungry. On
impulse, I accepted graciously and ate voraciously. Next thing
I knew, I was enjoying meat regularly again. And as often as
possible, it was, and continues to be, meat earned the good
old-fashioned hard way—by hunting our continent's increasingly abundant deer and elk.

Increasingly abundant thanks primarily to modern wildlife
management—which, like it or not, is a product of and almost
totally dependent upon hunting.

By the late 1800s, due to habitat plowed under by settlers
and an ongoing and unregulated slaughter by market shooters
(these were not hunters), North America's cervid populations
had been reduced to an all-time low, most species being
shoved hard against extinction, a few subspecies (Merriam
and Eastern elk, for two sad examples) pushed right over the
edge into oblivion. It was no "animal rights" group, but the
aforementioned  hunter-naturalist-conservationists—
Roosevelt et al—who sounded the first alarm, calling for the
enactment of stiff protective laws, vigorous enforcement of
those laws and the levying of special taxes on hunting and
hunting-related hard goods . . . taxes earmarked for funding
wildlife protection, restoration, management and habitat ac-
quisition programs.

America's elk and deer (and turkeys and black bears and
many other wild creatures great and small), together with a
good measure of our national pride, were snatched back from
the very brink. Today, North America supports the highest
numbers of elk and deer anyone now living has known. Or is
likely to know.

But hunting is killing; what of the killing?

Notwithstanding the emotional and uninformed claims of a
relative few strident anti-hunters to the contrary, after more
than thirty years of hunting I have not found the activity to
have desensitized me to death and suffering, much less to
have instilled in me a taste for blood and violence. It was, in

fact, fair-chase hunting that taught me to appreciate nature and led me, gradually but surely, to become an ardent student of nature. It takes one to know one, and being one myself, I like to believe I understand the collective psyche of hunters better than do the antis, and I have come to believe this: If a hunter is a bloodthirsty slob, he or she was so *a priori,* before and in spite of hunting, rather than because of it. Lord knows the hunter ranks are fat with slobs—but what corner of life is not today? Hunting is far from unique in that respect—it's just more (Day-Glo) visible.

But what of the prey, the victims of the hunt?

I have witnessed the nightmare of the slaughterhouse, held my nose while touring a poultry operation, watched claw-bound lobsters agonizing in a ten-gallon purgatory . . . and my hands have dripped red with the still-warm blood of deer, elk, caribou, smaller animals and birds. Having seen all this, were I forced to a choice by some wicked witch, rather than being transmogrified into a pig in a pen or reduced to a steer in a feedlot, I would beg to become a deer or an elk—born free, living wild and someday (it would be mine to hope) dying swiftly by arrow or bullet. (If getting shot doesn't sound all that appealing, consider the cervids' other options for departing this beautiful world . . . starving, freezing, being ripped apart by fang and claw, the slow torture of brainworm, a messy midnight rendezvous with a speeding Greyhound.)

Moreover, were wild animals magically given voice in the matter, I venture that even they would reluctantly endorse hunting—for without hunting and the financial, political and research support it provides, only a relative few cervids would even be here today, or will be here tomorrow.

As to being subjected to the terror of the hunt—all members of the deer family evolved as prey species; nervous by nature, wound spring-tight, past masters of evasion. Since man has removed most of their natural predators from the wild, were deer and elk not hunted by human predators, they soon would devolve to little more than park and garden pests—something far less grand than the clever and elusive products of a harsh evolution they now are . . . creatures the very sight of which, even given today's relatively high numbers, is so rare, fleeting and sublime that it quickens the appreciative viewer's pulse. Until the day we as a nation become unselfish enough to endorse the re-introduction of large natural predators— wolves and grizzly bears—we're stuck with the human hunter as a necessary management tool.

If hunting were banned or even unwisely limited, as the misnamed "animal welfare" faction would so have it, rather than seeing gains in the weal of our wildlife, we would see (as those who have been watching have seen in past "preservation" experiments at Grand Canyon and elsewhere) a rapid overpopulation and its horrific Malthusian upshots—increased collisions with automobiles, disease, genetic decline, overgrazing, eventual mass starvation—general misery all around. No matter what one thinks of hunting, to attack it broadside and indiscriminately, as is the fad in California, New Jersey, Rhode Island and a growing number of urban elsewheres in America today, is to threaten the very lifeblood of modern wildlife management and, consequently, to imperil wildlife itself.

If it ain't broke, don't fix it.

Hunting ain't broke, but that's not to say it doesn't have some low tires, a grinding gear or two, a few loose spokes. What can we, all of us who care—hunters, nonhunters and antis alike—do to tune up modern hunting while at the same time assuring for our posterity a plenitude and diversity of wildlife?

We who call ourselves hunters can start by examining our personal motives for walking about with bows or guns, looking to kill. We can, we *must,* police our own ranks—our friends and ourselves included and especially—and take a hard line to excise the slob-hunter cancer that taints, weakens and threatens— eventually, possibly—to destroy hunting.

(Who, exactly, is this infamous "slob hunter"? He is variously a cruise-around road shooter, an armed drunk, a slovenly litterer, a poacher, a flagrant trespasser, an enthusiastic cheat—in short, a self-serving bozo who no doubt performs similarly in nonhunting endeavors as well . . . parking in the handicapped zone at the post office, cutting in line at the market check-out, running stop signs, letting his fat, well-fed housecats roam loose to prey upon the neighborhood songbirds and small wildlife. The point is, he's not just a slob *hunter,* but an *all-around* slob.)

Real hunters must support mandatory hunter safety and ethics education and help to make it increasingly effective. We can lobby for more and more strenuous game law enforcement, swifter justice and stiffer penalties for violators. We must strive to shape a strong example for today's young people who may become tomorrow's hunters—or, perhaps, should we fail them—anti-hunters. In short, we need a cleaner, leaner, more athletic hunting paradigm.

Nonhunters can keep open minds and try to understand that slob hunters, in all their perverted and highly visible forms, neither speak nor act for the majority of hunters, and that the antis—like the worst of preachers and politicians—too often are dissemblers waging a dirty fight. (A primary reason the "animal rights" faction has made such progress of late is the timidity of the media, in particular tee-vee and general-interest magazines, which give the howling antis all the ink and air time they want, but fear to let the other side voice its opinion . . . or, should they occasionally pretend to do so, intentionally seek out a weak and unpolished voice.)

Finally, anti-hunter/animal welfare folk, if their true interest is in fact the long-term well-being of wild creatures rather than, as it appears from here, merely wishing to impose *their* moral code on *me,* can try to set aside their emotionally clouded and myopic disdain for hunting and hunters in favor of doing what is necessary to help wildlife in the long run. Cripple or destroy hunting, and you cripple or destroy wildlife's major—in some cases only—pillar of support.

Done right, hunting is as traditional and natural as making love (another unpopular activity in some puritanical circles). The keys to its continued acceptance by a largely urban and nonhunting public are education, responsibility and sensitivity. Deer and elk are not mere animated targets, and hunting them entails far more than a trip to the meat market. Just so.

To cadge an Ed Abbey line: If there's anyone still present whom I've failed to insult, I apologize.

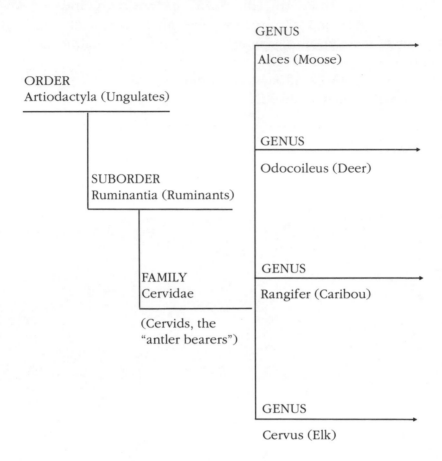

GENUS
Alces (Moose)

ORDER
Artiodactyla (Ungulates)

GENUS
Odocoileus (Deer)

SUBORDER
Ruminantia (Ruminants)

GENUS
Rangifer (Caribou)

FAMILY
Cervidae

(Cervids, the
"antler bearers")

GENUS
Cervus (Elk)

# Taxonomy of the North American Deer Family

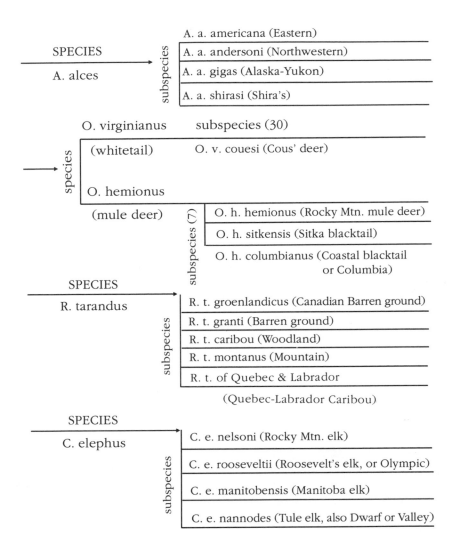

SPECIES
A. alces — subspecies

A. a. americana (Eastern)
A. a. andersoni (Northwestern)
A. a. gigas (Alaska-Yukon)
A. a. shirasi (Shira's)

species

O. virginianus    subspecies (30)
(whitetail)    O. v. couesi (Cous' deer)

O. hemionus
(mule deer) — subspecies (7)

O. h. hemionus (Rocky Mtn. mule deer)
O. h. sitkensis (Sitka blacktail)
O. h. columbianus (Coastal blacktail
                        or Columbia)

SPECIES
R. tarandus — subspecies

R. t. groenlandicus (Canadian Barren ground)
R. t. granti (Barren ground)
R. t. caribou (Woodland)
R. t. montanus (Mountain)
R. t. of Quebec & Labrador
        (Quebec-Labrador Caribou)

SPECIES
C. elephus — subspecies

C. e. nelsoni (Rocky Mtn. elk)
C. e. rooseveltii (Roosevelt's elk, or Olympic)
C. e. manitobensis (Manitoba elk)
C. e. nannodes (Tule elk, also Dwarf or Valley)

# Appendix B:

# DEER AND ELK CONSERVATION GROUPS

Like it or not, the only groups working directly—raising money and putting it on the ground where it counts—to help the various deer species are strongly hunter-based. Of these, I know quite a lot about one, a little something about another two.

🦌

**The Rocky Mountain Elk Foundation:** P.O. Box 8249, Missoula, MT 59807; phone 1-800-CALL-ELK.

The Rocky Mountain Elk Foundation was chartered in 1984 as a nonprofit conservation organization, and presently (winter 1990–91) has a membership of some fifty-five thousand. Many or most of this number, like myself, were drawn in by the group's classy and widely respected journal, *Bugle,* an average 175,000 copies of which are distributed quarterly through the mail to members and via newsstand sales. The editors, Lance Schelvan and Dan Crockett, select articles intended not just to entertain, but also to enlighten, educate and strengthen the outdoor ethics of their readers. Natural history, wildlife and habitat management essays regularly appear alongside hunting yarns. *Bugle* contains lots of color, both photos and art, and is a masterpiece of a magazine.

While the majority (an estimated ninety-five percent) of its members are conservation-minded hunters, the RMEF is balanced by a significant contingent of nonhunters. The foundation's official mission is "to raise funds for the direct benefit of elk, other wildlife and their habitat," and their good works are, as the old journalist's cliché would have it, far too numerous to list here. In a nutshell, though . . .

Traditional project categories include habitat enhancement, conservation education, land conservation, research and management. To date, RMEF has raised and put to work more than fifteen million dollars in these five critical areas. A hardworking and effective outfit it is—and their Missoula visitor's center boasts one of the most impressive collections of elk antlers and art available for free public viewing anywhere.

For those who wish to become locally involved, primarily by helping to organize and stage annual fund-raising banquets, there are some two hundred RMEF chapters scattered across the U.S. and Canada, with more sprouting up all the time.

An annual individual Supporting membership in the Rocky Mountain Elk Foundation is a tax-deductible $25, which includes four issues of *Bugle* and eight of *Wapiti,* RMEF's excellent newsletter.

**The Mule Deer Foundation:** P.O. Box 991168, Redding, CA 96099; phone 1-800-344-BUCK.

Young and as yet unproven, the Mule Deer Foundation—essentially a Rocky Mountain Elk Foundation clone (which is no disparagement)—seems to be on the right track. The premiere issue of its semi-annual magazine, *Mule Deer,* published in the fall of 1990, is attractive, with lots of color and a mix of hunting, natural history and management articles. I have not yet seen a copy of the group's newsletter, *Mule Deer Insights.* Both are included with an annual tax-deductible Full membership of $25.

Like the RMEF, the MDF uses local chapter banquets and a big annual convention as means of getting members together for socializing, education and fund-raising. A couple of the MDF's fledgling projects have been to fund a controlled burn in California (controlled, or "prescribed" burning of aspens, oak brush and other important winter wildlife foods are conducted by the U.S.F.S. and many state wildlife agencies to improve the browse-producing capabilities of critical big game habitat, most often on public lands; done right, they work), and to help customize an "undercover truck" for the Nevada Department of Wildlife, to be used in putting the sneak on and nabbing poachers and other game law violators.

**Whitetails Unlimited:** P.O. Box 422, Sturgeon Bay, WI 54235; phone 414/743-6777.

Founded in 1982, WTU now has a membership approaching forty thousand, the overwhelming majority of whom reside in the midwestern and northeastern states—which should come as no great surprise, since that's also where the preponderance of whitetails hang out. From WTU's published mission statement . . .

> The specific purposes of Whitetails Unlimited, Inc., shall be to (1) support programs which ensure the present and future well-being of the white-tailed deer and its habitat, (2) educate the general public on the importance of sound conservation practices, (3) promote compatibility between white-tailed deer populations and human landuse practices, (4) aid and financially support research on the white-tailed deer, and (5) facilitate a tele-communication and database system for indexed information pertaining to the white-tailed deer.

(A note for fellow pedantic grammarians: You've probably noticed that WTU embraces the noun "whitetail" in the con-joined form, but hyphenates the adjective "white-tailed." This is strictly correct. But it's also confusing—which is why current journalistic consensus, mine in particular, keeps the whitetail's tail firmly attached to its body no matter the part of speech it happens to be playing at the moment.)

Five times a year, WTU publishes *The Deer Trail*, thinner and less colorful than either *Bugle* or *Mule Deer*, but a nice little magazine nonetheless. Along with a subscription to *The Deer Trail,* a tax-deductible $25 annual WTU membership also includes a four-page monthly newsletter, "Chapter Connections."

In summary, my conviction is that if you hunt deer or elk, you are morally obligated to support one or more of the above hunter-conservation groups.

Records of North American
Big Game

BOONE AND CROCKETT CLUB

P.O. Box 547
Dumfries, VA 22026

Minimum Score: Awards All-time
360     375

TYPICAL
AMERICAN ELK (WAPITI)

DETAIL OF POINT
MEASUREMENT

| | Abnormal Points | |
|---|---|---|
| | Right Antler | Left Antler |
| | | |
| | | |
| | | |
| | | |
| E. Total of Lengths of Abnormal Points | | |

| SEE OTHER SIDE FOR INSTRUCTIONS | | | | Column 1 | Column 2 | Column 3 | Column 4 |
|---|---|---|---|---|---|---|---|
| A. No. Points on Right Antler | | No. Points on Left Antler | | Spread Credit | Right Antler | Left Antler | Difference |
| B. Tip to Tip Spread | | C. Greatest Spread | | | | | |
| D. Inside Spread of Main Beams | | (Credit May Equal But Not Exceed Longer Antler) | | | | | |
| F. Length of Main Beam | | | | | | | |
| G-1. Length of First Point | | | | | | | |
| G-2. Length of Second Point | | | | | | | |
| G-3. Length of Third Point | | | | | | | |
| G-4. Length of Fourth (Royal) Point | | | | | | | |
| G-5. Length of Fifth Point | | | | | | | |
| G-6. Length of Sixth Point, If Present | | | | | | | |
| G-7. Length of Seventh Point, If Present | | | | | | | |
| H-1. Circumference at Smallest Place Between First and Second Points | | | | | | | |
| H-2. Circumference at Smallest Place Between Second and Third Points | | | | | | | |
| H-3. Circumference at Smallest Place Between Third and Fourth Points | | | | | | | |
| H-4. Circumference at Smallest Place Between Fourth and Fifth Points | | | | | | | |
| TOTALS | | | | | | | |

| Enter Total of Columns 1, 2, and 3 | | Exact Locality Where Killed: | |
|---|---|---|---|
| Subtract Column 4 | | Date Killed: | By Whom Killed: |
| Subtotal | | Present Owner: | |
| Subtract (E) Total of Lengths of Abn. Points | | Guide Name and Address: | |
| FINAL SCORE | | Remarks: | |

165

I certify that I have measured the above trophy on _____ 19 _____

at (address) _____ City _____ State _____
and that these measurements and data are, to the best of my knowledge and belief, made in accordance with the
instructions given.

Witness: _____ Signature _____

                                         B&C OFFICIAL MEASURER

                                                                          I.D. Number

## INSTRUCTIONS FOR MEASURING TYPICAL AMERICAN ELK (WAPITI)

All measurements must be made with a 1/4-inch flexible steel tape to the nearest one-eighth of an inch. Wherever
it is necessary to change direction of measurement, mark a control point and swing tape at this point. (Note: a
flexible steel cable can be used to measure points and main beams only.) Enter fractional figures in eighths,
without reduction. Official measurements cannot be taken until the antlers have dried for at least 60 days after
the animal was killed.

A. Number of Points on Each Antler: to be counted a point, the projection must be at least one inch long, with
length exceeding width at one inch or more of length. All points are measured from tip of point to nearest edge
of beam as illustrated. Beam tip is counted as a point but not measured as a point.

B. Tip to Tip Spread is measured between tips of main beams.

C. Greatest Spread is measured between perpendiculars at a right angle to the center line of the skull at widest
part, whether across main beams or points.

D. Inside Spread of Main Beams is measured at a right angle to the center line of the skull at widest point
between main beams. Enter this measurement again as Spread Credit if it is less than or equal to the length of
longer antler; if longer, enter longer antler length for Spread Credit.

E. Total of Lengths of all Abnormal Points: Abnormal Points are those non-typical in location (such as points
originating from a point or from bottom or sides of main beam) or pattern (extra points, not generally paired).
Measure in usual manner and record in appropriate blanks.

F. Length of Main Beam is measured from lowest outside edge of burr over outer curve to the most distant point of
what is, or appears to be, the main beam. The point of beginning is that point on the burr where the center line
along the outer curve of the beam intersects the burr, then following generally the line of the illustration.

G. 1-2-3-4-5-6-7  Length of Normal Points: Normal points project from the top or front of the main beam in the
general pattern illustrated. They are measured from nearest edge of main beam over outer curve to tip. Lay the
tape along the outer curve of the beam so that the top edge of the tape coincides with the top edge of the beam
on both sides of point to determine the baseline for point measurement. Record point length in appropriate
blanks.

H. 1-2-3-4  Circumferences are taken as detailed for each measurement.

                       * * * * * * * * * * * * * * * * * * *

### FAIR CHASE STATEMENT FOR ALL HUNTER-TAKEN TROPHIES

To make use of the following methods shall be deemed as UNFAIR CHASE and unsportsmanlike, and any trophy
obtained by use of such means is disqualified from entry.

    I. Spotting or herding game from the air, followed by landing in its vicinity for pursuit;

    II. Herding or pursuing game with motor-powered vehicles;

    III. Use of electronic communications for attracting, locating or observing game, or guiding the
        hunter to such game;

    IV. Hunting game confined by artificial barriers, including escape-proof fencing; or hunting game
        transplanted solely for the purpose of commercial shooting.

                       * * * * * * * * * * * * * * * * * * *

I certify that the trophy scored on this chart was not taken in UNFAIR CHASE as defined above by the Boone
and Crockett Club. I further certify that it was taken in full compliance with local game laws of the
state, province, or territory.

Date _____  Signature of Hunter _____

                                                     (Have signature notarized by a Notary Public)

OFFICIAL SCORING SYSTEM FOR NORTH AMERICAN BIG GAME TROPHIES

Records of North American                                                      P.O. Box 547
Big Game                          BOONE AND CROCKETT CLUB              Dumfries, VA 22026

| Minimum Score: | Awards | All-time | | Kind of Caribou _____ |
|---|---|---|---|---|
| barren ground | 375 | 400 | CARIBOU | |
| mountain | 360 | 390 | | |
| Quebec-Labrador | 365 | 375 | | |
| woodland | 265 | 295 | | |
| Central Canada | | | | |
| barren ground | 330 | 345 | | |

*DETAIL OF POINT MEASUREMENT*

| SEE OTHER SIDE FOR INSTRUCTIONS | | Column 1 | Column 2 | Column 3 | Column 4 |
|---|---|---|---|---|---|
| | | Spread Credit | Right Antler | Left Antler | Difference |
| A. Tip to Tip Spread | | | | | |
| B. Greatest Spread | | | | | |
| C. Inside Spread of Main Beams | (Credit May Equal But Not Exceed Longer Antler) | | | | |
| D. Number of Points on Each Antler Excluding Brows | | | | | |
| Number of Points on Each Brow | | | | | |
| E. Length of Main Beam | | | | | |
| F-1. Length of Brow Palm or First Point | | | | | |
| F-2. Length of Bez or Second Point | | | | | |
| F-3. Length of Rear Point, If Present | | | | | |
| F-4. Length of Second Longest Top Point | | | | | |
| F-5. Length of Longest Top Point | | | | | |
| G-1. Width of Brow Palm | | | | | |
| G-2. Width of Top Palm | | | | | |
| H-1. Circumference at Smallest Place Between Brow and Bez Points | | | | | |
| H-2. Circumference at Smallest Place Between Bez and Rear Point, If Present | | | | | |
| H-3. Circumference at Smallest Place Before First Top Point | | | | | |
| H-4. Circumference at Smallest Place Between Two Longest Top Palm Points | | | | | |
| TOTALS | | | | | |

| Enter Total of Columns 1, 2, and 3 | | Exact Locality Where Killed: | |
|---|---|---|---|
| | | Date Killed: | By Whom Killed: |
| Subtract Column 4 | | Present Owner: | |
| FINAL SCORE | | Guide Name and Address: | |
| | | Remarks: | |

I certify that I have measured the above trophy on _____ 19 _____

at (address) _____ City _____ State _____
and that these measurements and data are, to the best of my knowledge and belief, made in accordance with the
instructions given.

Witness: _____ Signature _____

B&C OFFICIAL MEASURER  ☐ ☐ ☐ ☐

I.D. Number

## INSTRUCTIONS FOR MEASURING CARIBOU

All measurements must be made with a 1/4-inch flexible steel tape to the nearest one-eighth of an inch. Wherever
it is necessary to change direction of measurement, mark a control point and swing tape at this point. (Note: a
flexible steel cable can be used to measure points and main beams only.) Enter fractional figures in eighths,
without reduction. Official measurements cannot be taken until antlers have dried for at least 60 days after the
animal was killed.

A. Tip to Tip Spread is measured between tips of main beams.
B. Greatest Spread is measured between perpendiculars at a right angle to the center line of the skull at widest
part, whether across main beams or points.
C. Inside Spread of Main Beams is measured at a right angle to the center line of the skull at widest point
between main beams. Enter this measurement again as Spread Credit if it is less than or equal to the length of
longer antler; if longer, enter longer antler length for Spread Credit.
D. Number of Points on Each Antler: To be counted a point, a projection must be at least one-half inch long,
with length exceeding width at the point of measurement. Beam tip is counted as a point but not measured as a
point. There are no "abnormal" points in caribou.
E. Length of Main Beam is measured from lowest outside edge of burr over outer curve to the most distant point of
what is, or appears to be, the main beam. The point of beginning is that point on the burr where the center line
along the outer curve of the beam intersects the burr.
F. 1-2-3 Length of Points are measured from nearest edge of beam on the shortest line over outer curve to tip.
Lay the tape along the outer curve of the beam so that the top edge of the tape coincides with the top edge of
the beam on both sides of point to determine the baseline for point measurement. Record point lengths in
appropriate blanks.
F. 4-5 Length of Points are measured from the tip of the point to the top of the beam, then at a right angle to
the lower edge of beam. The Second Longest Top Point cannot be a point branch of the Longest Top Point.
G-1 Width of Brow is measured in a straight line from top edge to lower edge, as illustrated, with measurement
line at a right angle to main axis of brow.
G-2 Width of Top Palm is measured from midpoint of lower rear edge of main beam to midpoint of a dip between
points, at widest part of palm. The line of measurement begins and ends at midpoints of palm edges, which gives
credit for palm thickness.
H. 1-2-3-4 Circumferences are taken as described for measurements. If brow point is missing, take H-1 at
smallest point between burr and bez point. If rear point is missing, take H-2 and H-3 measurements at smallest
place between bez and first top point. Do not depress the tape into any dips of the palm or main beam.

* * * * * * * * * * * * * * * * * *

### FAIR CHASE STATEMENT FOR ALL HUNTER-TAKEN TROPHIES

To make use of the following methods shall be deemed as UNFAIR CHASE and unsportsmanlike, and any trophy
obtained by use of such means is disqualified from entry.

I.  Spotting or herding game from the air, followed by landing in its vicinity for pursuit;

II.  Herding or pursuing game with motor-powered vehicles;

III.  Use of electronic communications for attracting, locating or observing game, or guiding the
hunter to such game;

IV.  Hunting game confined by artificial barriers, including escape-proof fencing; or hunting game
transplanted solely for the purpose of commercial shooting.

* * * * * * * * * * * * * * * * * *

I certify that the trophy scored on this chart was not taken in UNFAIR CHASE as defined above by the Boone
and Crockett Club. I further certify that it was taken in full compliance with local game laws of the
state, province, or territory.

Date _____ Signature of Hunter _____

(Have signature notarized by a Notary Public)

OFFICIAL SCORING SYSTEM FOR NORTH AMERICAN BIG GAME TROPHIES

| Records of North American Big Game | BOONE AND CROCKETT CLUB | P.O. Box 547 Dumfries, VA 22026 |
|---|---|---|

Minimum Score: Awards All-time        Kind of Moose _____
Alaska-Yukon   210    224       MOOSE
Canada        185    195
Wyoming      140    155

DETAIL OF POINT MEASUREMENT

| SEE OTHER SIDE FOR INSTRUCTIONS | Column 1 | Column 2 | Column 3 | Column 4 |
|---|---|---|---|---|
| | | Right Antler | Left Antler | Difference |
| A. Greatest Spread | | | | |
| B. Number of Abnormal Points on Both Antlers | | | | |
| C. Number of Normal Points | | | | |
| D. Width of Palm | | | | |
| E. Length of Palm Including Brow Palm | | | | |
| F. Circumference of Beam at Smallest Place | | | | |
| TOTALS | | | | |

| Enter Total of Columns 1, 2, and 3 | | Exact Locality Where Killed: | |
|---|---|---|---|
| Subtract Column 4 | | Date Killed: | By Whom Killed: |
| FINAL SCORE | | Present Owner: | |
| | | Guide Name and Address: | |
| | | Remarks: | |

I certify that I have measured the above trophy on _____ 19 _____

at (Address) _____ (City) _____ (State) _____

and that these measurements and data are, to the best of my knowledge and belief, made in accordance with the

instructions given.

Witness: _____ Signature: _____

B&C OFFICIAL MEASURER    ☐ ☐ ☐ ☐

I.D. Number

## INSTRUCTIONS FOR MEASURING MOOSE

All measurements must be made with a 1/4-inch flexible steel tape to the nearest one-eighth of an inch. Enter fractional figures in eighths, without reduction. Official measurements cannot be taken until antlers have dried for at least sixty days after animal was killed.

A.  Greatest Spread is measured between perpendiculars in a straight line at a right angle to the center line of the skull.

B.  Number of Abnormal Points on Both Antlers: Abnormal points are those projections originating from normal points or from the upper or lower palm surface, or from the inner edge of palm (see illustration). Abnormal points must be at least one inch long, with length exceeding width at one inch or more of length.

C.  Number of Normal Points: Normal points originate from the outer edge of palm. To be counted a point, a projection must be at least one inch long, with the length exceeding width at one inch or more of length.

D.  Width of Palm is taken in contact with the under surface of palm, at a right angle to the length of palm measurement line. The line of measurement should begin and end at the midpoint of the palm edge, which gives credit for the desirable character of palm thickness.

E.  Length of Palm Including Brow Palm is taken in contact with the surface along the underside of the palm, parallel to the inner edge, from dips between points at the top to dips between points (if present) at the bottom. If a bay is present, measure across the open bay if the proper line of measurement, parallel to inner edge, follows this path. The line of measurement should begin and end at the midpoint of the palm edge, which gives credit for the desirable character of palm thickness.

F.  Circumference of Beam at Smallest Place is taken as illustrated.


* * * * * * * * * * * * * * * * * *


### FAIR CHASE STATEMENT FOR ALL HUNTER-TAKEN TROPHIES

To make use of the following methods shall be deemed as UNFAIR CHASE and unsportsmanlike, and any trophy obtained by use of such means is disqualified from entry.

I.  Spotting or herding game from the air, followed by landing in its vicinity for pursuit;

II.  Herding or pursuing game with motor-powered vehicles;

III.  Use of electronic communications for attracting, locating or observing game, or guiding the hunter to such game;

IV.  Hunting game confined by artificial barriers, including escape-proof fencing; or hunting game transplanted solely for the purpose of commercial shooting.


* * * * * * * * * * * * * * * * * *


I certify that the trophy scored on this chart was not taken in UNFAIR CHASE as defined above by the Boone and Crockett Club. I further certify that it was taken in full compliance with local game laws of the state, province, or territory.

Date: _____   Signature of Hunter: _____

(Have Signature Notarized by a Notary Public)

OFFICIAL SCORING SYSTEM FOR NORTH AMERICAN BIG GAME TROPHIES

| Records of North American Big Game | BOONE AND CROCKETT CLUB | P.O. Box 547 Dumfries, VA 22026 |
|---|---|---|

| Minimum Score: | Awards | All-time | | | |
|---|---|---|---|---|---|
| whitetail | 160 | 170 | TYPICAL | Kind of Deer _____ | |
| Coues' | 100 | 110 | WHITETAIL AND COUES' DEER | | |

DETAIL OF POINT MEASUREMENT

| | Abnormal Points | |
|---|---|---|
| | Right Antler | Left Antler |
| | | |
| | | |
| | | |
| | | |
| E. Total of Lengths of Abnormal Points | | |

| SEE OTHER SIDE FOR INSTRUCTIONS | | | | Column 1 | Column 2 | Column 3 | Column 4 |
|---|---|---|---|---|---|---|---|
| | | | | Spread Credit | Right Antler | Left Antler | Difference |
| A. No. Points on Right Antler | | No. Points on Left Antler | | | | | |
| B. Tip to Tip Spread | | C. Greatest Spread | | | | | |
| D. Inside Spread of Main Beams | | (Credit May Equal But Not Exceed Longer Antler) | | | | | |
| F. Length of Main Beam | | | | | | | |
| G-1. Length of First Point, If Present | | | | | | | |
| G-2. Length of Second Point | | | | | | | |
| G-3. Length of Third Point | | | | | | | |
| G-4. Length of Fourth Point, If Present | | | | | | | |
| G-5. Length of Fifth Point, If Present | | | | | | | |
| G-6. Length of Sixth Point, If Present | | | | | | | |
| G-7. Length of Seventh Point, If Present | | | | | | | |
| H-1. Circumference at Smallest Place Between Burr and First Point | | | | | | | |
| H-2. Circumference at Smallest Place Between First and Second Points | | | | | | | |
| H-3. Circumference at Smallest Place Between Second and Third Points | | | | | | | |
| H-4. Circumference at Smallest Place Between Third and Fourth Points | | | | | | | |
| TOTALS | | | | | | | |

| Enter Total of Columns 1, 2, and 3 | | Exact Locality Where Killed: | |
|---|---|---|---|
| Subtract Column 4 | | Date Killed: | By Whom Killed: |
| Subtotal | | Present Owner: | |
| Subtract (E) Total of Lengths of Abn. Points | | Guide Name and Address: | |
| FINAL SCORE | | Remarks: | |

I certify that I have measured the above trophy on _____ 19 _____

at (address) _____ City _____ State _____
and that these measurements and data are, to the best of my knowledge and belief, made in accordance with the
instructions given.

Witness: _____ Signature: _____

B&C OFFICIAL MEASURER   [   |   |   |   ]

I.D. Number

## INSTRUCTIONS FOR MEASURING TYPICAL WHITETAIL AND COUES' DEER

All measurements must be made with a 1/4-inch flexible steel tape to the nearest one-eighth of an inch. Wherever
it is necessary to change direction of measurement, mark a control point and swing tape at this point. (Note: a
flexible steel cable can be used to measure points and main beams only.) Enter fractional figures in eighths,
without reduction. Official measurements cannot be taken until antlers have dried for at least 60 days after the
animal was killed.

A. Number of Points on Each Antler: to be counted a point, the projection must be at least one inch long, with
the length exceeding width at one inch or more of length. All points are measured from tip of point to nearest
edge of beam as illustrated. Beam tip is counted as a point but not measured as a point.

B. Tip to Tip Spread is measured between tips of main beams.

C. Greatest Spread is measured between perpendiculars at a right angle to the center line of the skull at widest
part, whether across main beams or points.

D. Inside Spread of Main Beams is measured at a right angle to the center line of the skull at widest point
between main beams. Enter this measurement again as the Spread Credit if it is less than or equal to the length
of longer antler; if longer, enter longer antler length for Spread Credit.

E. Total of Lengths of all Abnormal Points: Abnormal Points are those non-typical in location (such as points
originating from a point or from bottom or sides of main beam) or extra points beyond the normal pattern of
points. Measure in usual manner and enter in appropriate blanks.

F. Length of Main Beam is measured from lowest outside edge of burr over outer curve to the most distant point of
what is, or appears to be, the main beam. The point of beginning is that point on the burr where the center line
along the outer curve of the beam intersects the burr, then following generally the line of the illustration.

G. 1-2-3-4-5-6-7 Length of Normal Points: Normal points project from the top of the main beam. They are
measured from nearest edge of main beam over outer curve to tip. Lay the tape along the outer curve of the beam
so that the top edge of the tape coincides with the top edge of the beam on both sides of the point to determine
the baseline for point measurements. Record point lengths in appropriate blanks.

H. 1-2-3-4 Circumferences are taken as detailed for each measurement. If brow point is missing, take H-1 and
H-2 at smallest place between burr and G-2. If G-4 is missing, take H-4 halfway between G-3 and tip of main
beam.

* * * * * * * * * * * * * * * * * *

### FAIR CHASE STATEMENT FOR ALL HUNTER-TAKEN TROPHIES

To make use of the following methods shall be deemed as UNFAIR CHASE and unsportsmanlike, and any trophy obtained
by use of such means is disqualified from entry.

I. Spotting or herding game from the air, followed by landing in its vicinity for pursuit;

II. Herding or pursuing game with motor-powered vehicles;

III. Use of electronic communications for attracting, locating or observing game, or guiding the
hunter to such game;

IV. Hunting game confined by artificial barriers, including escape-proof fencing; or hunting game
transplanted solely for the purpose of commercial shooting.

* * * * * * * * * * * * * * * * * *

I certify that the trophy scored on this chart was not taken in UNFAIR CHASE as defined above by the Boone and
Crockett Club. I further certify that it was taken in full compliance with local game laws of the state,
province, or territory.

Date: _____ Signature of Hunter: _____

(Have signature notarized by a Notary Public)

## OFFICIAL SCORING SYSTEM FOR NORTH AMERICAN BIG GAME TROPHIES

Records of North American
Big Game

BOONE AND CROCKETT CLUB

P.O. Box 547
Dumfries, VA 22026

| Minimum Score: | Awards | All-time |
|---|---|---|
| mule | 185 | 195 |
| Columbia | 120 | 130 |
| Sitka | 100 | 108 |

TYPICAL
MULE AND BLACKTAIL DEER

Kind of Deer _____

DETAIL OF POINT MEASUREMENT

| | Abnormal Points | |
|---|---|---|
| | Right Antler | Left Antler |
| | | |
| | | |
| | | |
| | | |
| E. Total of Lengths of Abnormal Points | | |

| SEE OTHER SIDE FOR INSTRUCTIONS | | | | Column 1 | Column 2 | Column 3 | Column 4 |
|---|---|---|---|---|---|---|---|
| A. No. Points on Right Antler | | No. Points on Left Antler | | Spread Credit | Right Antler | Left Antler | Difference |
| B. Tip to Tip Spread | | C. Greatest Spread | | | | | |
| D. Inside Spread of Main Beams | | (Credit May Equal But Not Exceed Longer Antler) | | | | | |
| F. Length of Main Beam | | | | | | | |
| G-1. Length of First Point, If Present | | | | | | | |
| G-2. Length of Second Point | | | | | | | |
| G-3. Length of Third Point, If Present | | | | | | | |
| G-4. Length of Fourth Point, If Present | | | | | | | |
| H-1. Circumference at Smallest Place Between Burr and First Point | | | | | | | |
| H-2. Circumference at Smallest Place Between First and Second Points | | | | | | | |
| H-3. Circumference at Smallest Place Between Main Beam and Third Point | | | | | | | |
| H-4. Circumference at Smallest Place Between Second and Fourth Points | | | | | | | |
| TOTALS | | | | | | | |

| | | | |
|---|---|---|---|
| Enter Total of Columns 1, 2, and 3 | | Exact Locality Where Killed: | |
| Subtract Column 4 | | Date Killed: | By Whom Killed: |
| Subtotal | | Present Owner: | |
| Subtract (E) Total of Lengths of Abn. Points | | Guide Name and Address: | |
| FINAL SCORE | | Remarks: | |

I certify that I have measured the above trophy on _____ 19 _____

at (address) _____ City _____ State _____
and that these measurements and data are, to the best of my knowledge and belief, made in accordance with the
instructions given.

Witness: _____ Signature: _____

B&C OFFICIAL MEASURER [ ][ ][ ]

## INSTRUCTIONS FOR MEASURING TYPICAL MULE AND BLACKTAIL DEER

I.D. Number

All measurements must be made with a 1/4-inch flexible steel tape to the nearest one-eighth of an inch. Whereve
it is necessary to change direction of measurement, mark a control point and swing tape at this point. (Note: a
flexible steel cable can be used to take point and beam length measurements only.) Enter fractional figures in
eighths, without reduction. Official measurements cannot be taken until antlers have dried for at least 60 days
after the animal was killed.

A. Number of Points on Each Antler: to be counted a point, the projection must be at least one inch long, with
length exceeding width at one inch or more of length. All points are measured from tip of point to nearest edge
of beam as illustrated. Beam tip is counted as a point but not measured as a point.

B. Tip to Tip Spread is measured between tips of main beams.

C. Greatest Spread is measured between perpendiculars at a right angle to the center line of the skull at wides
part, whether across main beams or points.

D. Inside Spread of Main Beams is measured at a right angle to the center line of the skull at widest point
between main beams. Enter this measurement again as Spread Credit if it is less than or equal to the length of
longer antler; if longer, enter longer antler length for Spread Credit.

E. Total of Lengths of all Abnormal Points: Abnormal Points are those non-typical in location such as points
originating from a point (exception: G-3 originates from G-2 in perfectly normal fashion) or from bottom or sid
of main beam, or any points beyond the normal pattern of five (including beam tip) per antler. Measure each
abnormal point in usual manner and enter in appropriate blanks.

F. Length of Main Beam is measured from lowest outside edge of burr over outer curve to the most distant point
what is, or appears to be, the Main Beam. The point of beginning is that point on the burr where the center li
along the outer curve of the beam intersects the burr, then following generally the line of the illustration.

G. 1-2-3-4 Length of Normal Points: Normal points are the brow and the upper and lower forks as shown in the
illustration. They are measured from nearest edge of beam over outer curve to tip. Lay the tape along the out
curve of the beam so that the top edge of the tape coincides with the top edge of the beam on both sides of poi
to determine the baseline for point measurement. Record point lengths in appropriate blanks.

H. 1-2-3-4 Circumferences are taken as detailed for each measurement. If brow point is missing, take H-1 and
2 at smallest place between burr and G-2. If G-3 is missing, take H-3 halfway between the base and tip of seco
point. If G-4 is missing, take H-4 halfway between second point and tip of main beam.

\* \* \* \* \* \* \* \* \* \* \* \* \* \* \* \* \* \*

## FAIR CHASE STATEMENT FOR ALL HUNTER-TAKEN TROPHIES

To make use of the following methods shall be deemed as UNFAIR CHASE and unsportsmanlike, and any trophy obtain
by use of such means is disqualified from entry.

I. Spotting or herding game from the air, followed by landing in its vicinity for pursuit;

II. Herding or pursuing game with motor-powered vehicles;

III. Use of electronic communications for attracting, locating or observing game, or guiding the
hunter to such game;

IV. Hunting game confined by artificial barriers, including escape-proof fencing; or hunting game
transplanted solely for the purpose of commercial shooting.

\* \* \* \* \* \* \* \* \* \* \* \* \* \* \* \* \* \*

I certify that the trophy scored on this chart was not taken in UNFAIR CHASE as defined above by the Boone and
Crockett Club. I further certify that it was taken in full compliance with local game laws of the state,
province, or territory.

Date: _____ Signature of Hunter: _____

(Have signature notarized by a Notary Publi

# Bibliography

Abbey, Edward. *Desert Solitaire.* Tucson: University of Arizona Press, 1988.

Almy, Kathleen. "Lichens: Nature's Paintbox." *Sierra,* November/December 1988.

Anzelmo, Joan. Public Information Officer, Yellowstone National Park, Wyoming. Telephone interview with author, December 1988.

Attenborough, David. *The Living Planet.* Boston, Massachusetts: Little, Brown & Company, 1984.

Bergerud. A.T. "Caribou." *Big Game of North America: Ecology and Management.* Edited by John Schmidt and Douglas Gilbert. Harrisburgh, Pennsylvania: Stackpole Books, 1978.

Bird, Robert. Bureau Chief, Montana Department of Fish, Wildlife, and Parks. Telephone interview with author, December 1988.

Bubenik, Anthony B. Telephone interview and correspondence with author, 1988–89.

———."Proposals for Standardized Nomenclature for Bony Appendices in *Pecora,*" and "The Behaviorial Aspects of Antlerogenesis." In *Antler Development in Cervidae,* edited by Robert D. Brown. Kingsville, Texas: Caesar Kleberg Wildlife Research Institute, Texas A & I University, 1982.

———."Physiology." *Elk of North America: Ecology and Management.* Edited by Jack Ward Thomas and Dale E. Toweill. Harrisburgh, Pennsylvania: Stackpole Books, 1982.

———."Antlers," and "An Immodest Proposal." *Bugle: The Quarterly Journal of the Rocky Mountain Elk Foundation,* Fall 1988.

Bubenik, George A. Telephone interview and correspondence with author, 1988.

Bubenik, George A., and Anthony B. Bubenik. "Phylogeny and Ontogeny of Antlers and Neuro-Endocrine Regulation of the Antler Cycle—a Review." *Saugetierkundliche Mitteilungen (Mammalogical Informations),* Vol. 33, 1986.

Carron, Carey, District Wildlife Manager, Colorado Division of Wildlife, Bayfield, Colorado. Personal interviews with author, 1988.

Caton, John Dean. "Abnormal Deer Antlers from Texas." *American Naturalist,* No. 18, 1884. (As quoted in Goss, Richard J. *Deer Antlers.* New York: Academic Press, 1983.)

Chung, Kern. Korean antler dealer. Telephone interview with author, November 1988.

Clutton-Brock, Timothy, et al. *The Red Deer.* Chicago: University of Chicago Press, 1982.

Darwin, Charles. *The Origin of Species and The Descent of Man.* New York: The Modern Library (Random House, Inc.), no date.

Franzmann, Albert W. "Moose." *Big Game of North America: Ecology and Management.* Edited by John Schmidt and Douglas Gilbert. Harrisburgh, Pennsylvania: Stackpole Books, 1978.

Geist, Valerius. "On Speciation in Ice Age Mammals, with Special Reference to Cervids and Caprids." *The Canadian Journal of Zoology,* Vol. 65, 1987.

————."The Paradox of the Great Irish Stags." *Natural History,* March 1986. (Quoted here with the permission of *Natural History,* Vol. 95, No. 3; copyright The American Museum of Natural History, 1986.

————.Correspondence with author, 1988.

Geist, Valerius, and M. Bayer. "Sexual Dimorphism in the Cervidae and its Relation to Habitat." *The Journal of the Zoological Society of London,* No. 214, 1988.

Gibbons, George. "The Moose and the Man," in Ernest Thompson Seton's *Lives of Game Animals,* Vol. III. Garden City, New York: Doubleday, Doran & Company, 1927.

Gilbert, Douglas L. "Evolution and Taxonomy." *Big Game of North America: Ecology and Management.* Harrisburgh, Pennsylvania: Stackpole Books, 1978.

Goss, Richard J. *Deer Antlers: Regeneration, Function, and Evolution.* New York: Academic Press, 1983.

Gould, Stephen Jay. "The Origin and Function of 'Bizarre' Structures: Antler Size and Skull Size in the 'Irish Elk,' *Megaloceros Giganteus.*" *Evolution,* June 1974.

————."The Misnamed, Mistreated, and Misunderstood Irish Elk," and Epilogue. *Ever Since Darwin: Reflections in Natural History.* New York: W.W. Norton & Company, Inc., 1977.

————."Ten Thousand Acts of Kindness." *Natural History,* December 1988.

Griffin, Jim. Assistant manager, National Elk Refuge, Jackson, Wyoming. Telephone interview with author, November 1988.

Guthrie, A.B., Jr. *Big Sky, Fair Land: The Environmental Essays of A.B. Guthrie, Jr.* Edited by David Petersen. Flagstaff, Arizona: Northland Publishing Company, 1988.

———.Correspondence with author, November 1988.


Haigh, J.C. "Velveting." In *NAEBA News,* June, 1990.

Hale, Mason E. "Lichen." *Encyclopedia Americana.* Danbury, Connecticut, Grolier International, Inc., 1985.

Harrison, Jim. "The Tugboats of Costa Rica." In Smart, November/December 1989.


Luick, Jack R. "The Velvet Antler Industry." In *Antler Development in Cervidae,* edited by Robert D. Brown. Kingsville, Texas: Caesar Kleberg Wildlife Research Institute, Texas A & I University, 1983.


Malthus, Thomas. *An Essay on the Principle of Population.* London, 1798.

Muir, John. "Deer." In *Muir Among the Animals,* edited by Lisa Mighetto, San Francisco, California: Sierra Club Books, 1986. (Originally in *Our National Parks.* Boston: Houghton Mifflin, 1901.)


Nesbitt, William H., and Philip L. Wright, eds. *Boone and Crockett Club's Records of North American Big Game,* 8th edition. Dumfries, Virginia, 1981.

Nesbitt, William H., and Jack Reneau, eds. *Boone and Crockett Club's 19th Big Game Awards.* Dumfries, Virginia, 1986.

Newbrey, Jerrett. Telephone interview with author, September 1988.


Peacock, Doug. "Legend of A Killer Grizzly." In *American Country,* July 1987.

———.*Grizzly Years.* New York, Henry Holt: 1990.

Petersen, David L. "The Wyman Elk Ranch." *Mother Earth News.* March/April 1986.

———."A Prairie Goat Companion." *Mother Earth News.* November/December 1987.

———."Of Moose, *Megaloceros* and Miracles." *Mother Earth News.* March/April 1989.

———.*Among the Elk: Wilderness Images.* Flagstaff, Arizona: Northland Publishing, 1988.

Potter, Dale R. "Recreational Uses of Elk." In *Elk of North America: Ecology and Management,* edited by Jack Ward Thomas and Dale E. Toweill. Harrisburgh, Pennsylvania: Stackpole Books, 1982.

Rice, John. Executive Director, North American Elk Breeders Association. Personal conversation, September, 1990.

Rowe, J.P. "Inquisition." *Encyclopedia Americana,* No. 15. Danbury, Connecticut: Grolier International Inc., 1985.

Rozman, Ed. Personal correspondence and telephone interviews, July, 1990.

Rue, Leonard Lee III. *Sportsman's Guide to Game Animals.* New York: Harper & Row, 1968.

————.*The Deer of North America.* New York: Crown Publishers, 1978.

Ruch, Jim. "In My Opinion: From Montrose to Moscow, The Environment Is What Counts." *Colorado Wildlife,* December 1988.


Saunders, John J. "Crusades." *Encyclopedia Americana,* No. 8. Danbury, Connecticut: Grolier International Inc., 1985.

Schelvan, Lance. *Bugle* Magazine editor. Personal and telephone conversations, 1989–90.

Seton, Ernest Thompson. *Lives of Game Animals,* Vols. III and IV. Garden City, New York: Doubleday, Doran & Company, 1927–28.


Wilkinson, Todd. "Yellowstone Poaching War." *Defenders,* May/June 1988.

Wolfe, Gary J. "Population Dynamics of the Vermejo Park Elk Herd, with Special Reference to Trophy Management." Unpublished doctoral dissertation, Colorado State University, 1985.

————."The Relationship Between Age and Antler Development in Wapiti." *Antler Development in Cervidae,* edited by Robert D. Brown. Kingsville, Texas: Caesar Kleberg Wildlife Research Institute, Texas A & I University, 1982.

————."Old Elk, Trophy Elk." *Bugle: The Quarterly Journal of the Rocky Mountain Elk Foundation.* Fall 1984.

————."Antlers Away." *Bugle: The Quarterly Journal of the Rocky Mountain Elk Foundation.* Winter 1988/89.

————.Telephone interviews, personal interviews, and correspondence with author, 1986–89.

Wolfe, Gary J., and William R. Lance. "Locoweed Poisoning in a Northern New Mexico Elk Herd." *Journal of Range Management,* January 1984.

Wyman, Lou and Paula. The Wyman Elk Ranch, Craig, Colorado. Personal and telephone interviews with author, 1986 and 1988.


Zumbo, Jim. "The Biggest Elk Ever." *Bugle: The Quarterly Journal of the Rocky Mountain Elk Foundation.* Winter 1987–88.

DAVID PETERSEN is the author of four books of natural history, including *Among the Elk* (1988) and countless articles on outdoor subjects. He served as senior editor for *Mother Earth News* until 1990 and now lives in a small cabin with his wife, Carol, in the San Juan Mountains near Durango, Colorado.